The C to D of the London Underground

By

Polonius Kettle

www.fast-print.net/store.php

The C to D of the London Underground

A catalogue record for this book is available from the British Library

ISBN 978-178035-564-1

First published 2013 by
FASTPRINT PUBLISHING
Peterborough, England.

The C to D of the London Underground

The C to D of the London Underground tells you which London Tube carriage to board, by which door and on which side of the carriage to stand in order to be as close as possible to the exit at your destination station.

For example, you are on the Northern Line travelling southwards and wish to change at London Bridge for the Jubilee Line.

Look up:-

London Bridge,
Northern,
Direction From – North
Goal – Jubilee

You can now see that you need to be in...

Carriage 2 (from the front of the train) and next to...

Door 2 (from the front of the carriage) and on the left hand side (when facing front).

(The side is useful if the carriage is crowded.)

Please note that:-

a) Sometimes the accuracy of the Door number can depend on the whim of the driver who may not always stop at exactly the same point in some stations;

b) Some Carriages have three doors while others have four, so 4 can mean 3 and vice versa.

If you don't know from which end of a platform a train enters, just refer to the carriage side. The train will enter from the opposite of the carriage side, i.e. L means from the right and R from the left.

Acton Town

District **No of Carriages = 6**

Direction From – East
Previous Station – Chiswick Park

Goal	Carriage	Door	Side
Exit	2	1	R
Piccadilly (Eastwards)	2	1	R
Piccadilly (Westwards)	Any	Any	R

Direction From – West
Previous Station – Ealing Common

Goal	Carriage	Door	Side
Exit	5	4	R
Piccadilly (Eastwards)	Any	Any	R
Piccadilly (Westwards)	5	4	R

Piccadilly **No of Carriages = 6**

Direction From – East
Previous Station – Turnham Green

Goal	Carriage	Door	Side
District (Eastwards)	2	2	L
District (Westwards)	Any	Any	L
Exit	2	2	L

Direction From – West
Previous Station – South Ealing/Ealing Common
Platform 3

Goal	Carriage	Door	Side
District (Eastwards)	Any	Any	L
District (Westwards)	5	4	L
Exit	5	4	L

Aldgate

Circle

No of Carriages = 6

Direction From – North
Previous Station – Liverpool Street

Goal	Carriage	Door	Side
Exit	3	2	R
Exit	5	1	R
Metropolitan (North) Plat. 2	Any	Any	R
Metropolitan (North) Plat. 3	3	2	R
Metropolitan (North) Plat. 3	5	1	R

Direction From – South
Previous Station – Tower Hill

Goal	Carriage	Door	Side
Exit	1	4	R
Exit	3	2	R
Metropolitan (North) Plat. 2	1	4	R
Metropolitan (North) Plat. 2	3	2	R
Metropolitan (North) Plat. 3	Any	Any	R

Metropolitan *(Terminus)*

No of Carriages = 8

Direction From – North
Previous Station – Liverpool Street
Arrival at Platform 2

Goal	Carriage	Door	Side
Circle (Tower Hill)	Any	Any	L
Exit	4	3	L
Exit	5	4	L

Direction From – North
Previous Station – Liverpool Street
Arrival at Platform 3

Goal	Carriage	Door	Side
Circle (Tower Hill)	4	4	R
Circle (Tower Hill)	5	1	R
Exit	4	4	R
Exit	5	1	R

Aldgate East

District — **No of Carriages = 6**

Direction From – East
Previous Station – Whitechapel

Goal	Carriage	Door	Side
Exit (Toynbee Hall, High St & Leman St)	1	1	L
Exit (Whitechapel Art Gallery)	6	4	L
Hammersmith & City (To East)	Any	Any	L

Direction From – West
Previous Station – Tower Hill

Goal	Carriage	Door	Side
Exit (Toynbee Hall, High St & Leman St)	6	4	L
Exit (Whitechapel Art Gallery)	1	1	L
Hammersmith & City (To West)	6	4	L

Hammersvmith & City — **No of Carriages = 6**

Direction From – East
Previous Station – Whitechapel

Goal	Carriage	Door	Side
District	Any	Any	L
Exit (Toynbee Hall, High St & Leman St)	1	1	L
Exit (Whitechapel Art Gallery)	6	4	L

Direction From – West
Previous Station – Liverpool Street

Goal	Carriage	Door	Side
District (Westwards)	6	4	L
Exit (Toynbee Hall, High St & Leman St)	6	4	L
Exit (Whitechapel Art Gallery)	1	1	L

Alperton

Piccadilly — **No of Carriages = 6**

Direction From – North
Previous Station – Sudbury Town

Goal	Carriage	Door	Side
Exit	2	1	L

Direction From – South
Previous Station – Park Royal

Goal	Carriage	Door	Side
Exit	6	3	L

Amersham *(Terminus)*

Metropolitan **No of Carriages = 8**

Direction From – East
Previous Station – Chalfont & Latimer

Goal	Carriage	Door	Side
Exit (over bridge)	5	3	L
Rail (Northwards)	Any	Any	L

Angel

Northern **No of Carriages = 6**

Direction From – East
Previous Station – Old Street

Goal	Carriage	Door	Side
Exit	2	2	R

Direction From – West
Previous Station – King's Cross St. Pancras

Goal	Carriage	Door	Side
Exit	6	1/2	R

Archway

Northern **No of Carriages = 6**

Direction From – North
Previous Station – Highgate

Goal	Carriage	Door	Side
Exit	5	4	R

Direction From – South
Previous Station – Tufnell Park

Goal	Carriage	Door	Side
Exit	2	3	R

Arnos Grove

Piccadilly **No of Carriages = 6**

Direction From – North
Previous Station – Southgate

Goal	Carriage	Door	Side
Exit	4	4	L/R
Exit	3	3	L/R

Direction From – South
Previous Station – Bounds Green

Goal	Carriage	Door	Side
Exit	4	2	R
Exit	3	1	R

Arsenal

Piccadilly **No of Carriages = 6**

Direction From – North
Previous Station – Upper Holloway

Goal	Carriage	Door	Side
Exit	4	2	R

Direction From – South
Previous Station – Holloway Road

Goal	Carriage	Door	Side
Exit	3	2	R

Baker Street

Bakerloo **No of Carriages = 7**

Direction From – North
Previous Station – Marylebone

Goal	Carriage	Door	Side
Circle	4	3	L
Exit	1	3	L
Exit	4	3	L
Hammersmith & City	4	3	L
Jubilee South-Bound	1	3	L
Jubilee South-Bound	4	3	L
Jubilee South-Bound	6	4	L
Jubilee North-Bound	5	2	L
Metropolitan	1	3	L
Metropolitan	4	3	L

Baker Street *(cont...)*

Bakerloo *(cont...)* **No of Carriages = 7**
Direction From – South
Previous Station – Regent's Park

Goal	Carriage	Door	Side
Circle	3	4	R
Exit	2	3	R
Exit	3	4	R
Hammersmith & City	3	4	R
Jubilee	2	3	R
Jubilee North Bound	7	3	R
Metropolitan	3	4	R

Circle **No of Carriages = 6**
Direction From – East
Previous Station – Great Portland Street

Goal	Carriage	Door	Side
Bakerloo	5	4	L
Exit	5	4	L
Hammersmith & City	Any	Any	L
Jubilee	5	4	L
Metropolitan	5	4	L

Direction From – West
Previous Station – Edgware Road

Goal	Carriage	Door	Side
Bakerloo	1	Any	L
Bakerloo	3	3	L
Exit	1	Any	L
Hammersmith & City	Any	Any	L
Jubilee	1	Any	L
Jubilee	3	3	L
Metropolitan	1	Any	L

Hammersmith & City

No of Carriages = 6

Direction From – East
Previous Station – Great Portland Street

Goal	Carriage	Door	Side
Bakerloo	5	3	L
Circle	Any	Any	L
Exit	5	3	L
Jubilee	5	3	L
Metropolitan	5	5	L

Direction From – North West
Previous Station – Edgware Road

Goal	Carriage	Door	Side
Bakerloo	1	Any	L
Bakerloo	3	4	L
Circle	1	Any	L
Exit	1	Any	L
Jubilee	1	Any	L
Jubilee	3	4	L
Metropolitan	1	Any	L

Jubilee

No of Carriages = 7

Direction From – North
Previous Station – St John's Wood

Goal	Carriage	Door	Side
Bakerloo (North-Bound)	5	3	R
Bakerloo (South-Bound)	2	2/3	R
Bakerloo (South-Bound)	5	3	R
Bakerloo (South-Bound)	6	3	R
Circle	2	4	R
Exit	2	4	R
Hammersmith & City	2	4	R
Metropolitan	2	4	R

Baker Street *(cont...)*

Jubilee *(cont...)*

No of Carriages = 7

Direction From – South
Previous Station – Bond Street

Goal	Carriage	Door	Side
Bakerloo	1	2	L
Bakerloo (North-Bound)	5	2	L
Circle	2	4	L
Exit	2	4	L
Hammersmith & City	2	4	L
Metropolitan	2	4	L

Metropolitan

No of Carriages = 8

Direction From – East
Previous Station – Great Portland Street

Goal	Carriage	Door	Side
Bakerloo	5	1	L
Circle	6	4	L
Exit	6	4	L
Hammersmith & City	6	4	L
Jubilee	5	1	L

Direction From – North West
Previous Station – South Hampstead

Goal	Carriage	Door	Side
Bakerloo	5	1	L
Circle	2	3	L
Exit	2	3	L
Hammersmith & City	2	3	L
Jubilee	5	1	L

Direction From – North West
Previous Station – South Hampstead
(If terminating at Platforms 1 or 4)

Goal	Carriage	Door	Side
Bakerloo	3	4	L/R
Circle	1	2	L/R
Exit	1	2	L/R
Hammersmith & City	1	2	L/R
Jubilee	3	4	L/R

Balham

Northern — **No of Carriages = 6**

Direction From – North
Previous Station – Clapham South

Goal	Carriage	Door	Side
Exit	3	3	R

Direction From – South
Previous Station – Tooting Bec

Goal	Carriage	Door	Side
Exit	4	2	R

Bank

Central — **No of Carriages = 8**

Direction From – East
Previous Station – Liverpool Street

Goal	Carriage	Door	Side
District & Circle	3	2	R
District & Circle	6	2	R
DLR	3	2	R
DLR	6	2	R
Exit	7	3	R
Lift	1	1	R
Northern	6	2	R
Waterloo & City	3	2	R
Waterloo & City	7	3	R

Direction From – West
Previous Station – St. Paul's

Goal	Carriage	Door	Side
District & Circle	3	4	R
District & Circle	6	2	R
DLR	3	4	R
DLR	6	2	R
Exit	2	3	R
Lift	8	3	R
Northern	3	4	R
Waterloo & City	2	3	R
Waterloo & City	6	2	R

Bank *(cont...)*

Northern **No of Carriages = 6**

Direction From – North
Previous Station – Moorgate

Goal	Carriage	Door	Side
Central	6	4	L
Circle	1	1	L
District	1	1	L
DLR	1	2	L
DLR	3	2	L
Exit (Monument)	1	1	L
Exit (Bank)	6	4	L
Waterloo & City	6	4	L

Direction From – South
Previous Station – London Bridge

Goal	Carriage	Door	Side
Central	1	1	L
Circle	6	4	L
District	6	4	L
DLR	6	3	L
DLR	4	2	L
Exit (Monument)	6	4	L
Exit (Bank)	1	1	L
Waterloo & City	1	1	L

Waterloo & City *(Terminus)* **No of Carriages = 4**

Direction From – South
Previous Station – Waterloo

Goal	Carriage	Door	Side
Exit	1	1	L/R
Central	1	1	L/R
Northern	1	1	L/R
DLR	1	1	L/R
Monument	1	1	L/R

Barbican

Circle **No of Carriages = 6**

Direction From – East
Previous Station – Farringdon

Goal	Carriage	Door	Side
Exit	6	4	L

Direction From – West
Previous Station – Moorgate

Goal	Carriage	Door	Side
Exit	1	1	L

Metropolitan **No of Carriages = 8**

Direction From – East
Previous Station – Farringdon

Goal	Carriage	Door	Side
Exit	7	2	L

Direction From – West
Previous Station – Moorgate

Goal	Carriage	Door	Side
Exit	1	3	L

Hammersmith & City **No of Carriages = 6**

Direction From –East
Previous Station – Farringdon

Goal	Carriage	Door	Side
Exit	6	4	L

Direction From – West
Previous Station – Moorgate

Goal	Carriage	Door	Side
Exit	1	2	L

Barking

District **No of Carriages = 6**

Direction From – North East
Previous Station – Upney

Goal	Carriage	Door	Side
Exit	6	2	R
Rail	6	2	R
Rail	2	4	R

Direction From – South West
Previous Station – East Ham

Goal	Carriage	Door	Side
Exit	2	4	R
Rail	2	4	R
Rail	6	2	R

Hammersmith & City *(Terminus)* **No of Carriages = 6**

Direction From – South West
Previous Station – East Ham

Goal	Carriage	Door	Side
Exit	1	1	R
District	1	1	R
Rail	1	1	R

Barkingside

Central **No of Carriages = 8**

Direction From – North
Previous Station – Fairlop

Goal	Carriage	Door	Side
Exit (via Footbridge)	3	3	L

Direction From – South
Previous Station – Newbury Park

Goal	Carriage	Door	Side
Exit	4	2	L

Barons Court

District **No of Carriages = 6**

Direction From – East
Previous Station – West Kensington

Goal	Carriage	Door	Side
Exit	6	4	L
Piccadilly	Any	Any	L

Direction From – West
Previous Station – Hammersmith

Goal	Carriage	Door	Side
Exit	1	1	L
Piccadilly	Any	Any	L

Piccadilly **No of Carriages = 6**

Direction From – East
Previous Station – Earl's Court

Goal	Carriage	Door	Side
District	Any	Any	L
Exit	6	4	L

Direction From – West
Previous Station – Hammersmith

Goal	Carriage	Door	Side
District	Any	Any	L
Exit	1	1	L

Bayswater

District & **Circle** **No of Carriages = 6**

Direction From – North
Previous Station – Paddington

Goal	Carriage	Door	Side
Exit	5	1/2	L

Direction From – South
Previous Station – Notting Hill Gate

Goal	Carriage	Door	Side
Exit	2	3	L

Becontree

District **No of Carriages = 6**

Direction From – North East
Previous Station – Dagenham Heathway

Goal	Carriage	Door	Side
Exit	6	4	L

Direction From – South West
Previous Station – Upney

Goal	Carriage	Door	Side
Exit	1	1	L

Belsize Park

Northern **No of Carriages = 6**

Direction From – North
Previous Station – Hampstead

Goal	Carriage	Door	Side
Exit	4	2	R

Direction From – South
Previous Station – Chalk Farm

Goal	Carriage	Door	Side
Exit	3	1	R

Bermondsey

Jubilee **No of Carriages = 7**

Direction From – East
Previous Station – Canada Water

Goal	Carriage	Door	Side
Exit	2	4	R
Lift	1	3	R

Direction From – West
Previous Station – London Bridge

Goal	Carriage	Door	Side
Exit	5	1	R
Lift	5	1	R

Bethnal Green

Central — **No of Carriages = 8**

Direction From – East
Previous Station – Mile End

Goal	Carriage	Door	Side
Exit	1	1	L

Direction From – West
Previous Station – Liverpool Street

Goal	Carriage	Door	Side
Exit	1	1	L

Blackfriars

District & Circle — **No of Carriages = 6**

Direction From – East
Previous Station – Mansion House

Goal	Carriage	Door	Side
Exit	4	2	L
Rail	4	2	L
River Boat	4	2	L

Direction From – West
Previous Station – Temple

Goal	Carriage	Door	Side
Exit	3	1	L
Rail	3	1	L
River Boat	3	1	L

Blackhorse Road

Victoria — **No of Carriages = 8**

Direction From – East
Previous Station – Walthamstow Central

Goal	Carriage	Door	Side
Exit	5	1/2	R
Rail	5	1/2	R

Direction From – West
Previous Station – Tottenham Hale

Goal	Carriage	Door	Side
Exit	4	2	R
Rail	4	2	R

Bond Street

Central **No of Carriages = 8**

Direction From – East
Previous Station – Oxford Circus

Goal	Carriage	Door	Side
Exit	6	2	R
Jubilee	1	4	R

Direction From – West
Previous Station – Marble Arch

Goal	Carriage	Door	Side
Exit	1	2	R
Jubilee	6	2	R

Jubilee **No of Carriages = 7**

Direction From – North
Previous Station – Baker Street

Goal	Carriage	Door	Side
Central	4	2	R
Exit	4	2	R

Direction From – South
Previous Station – Green Park

Goal	Carriage	Door	Side
Central	4	3	R
Exit	4	3	R

Borough

Northern **No of Carriages = 6**

Direction From – North
Previous Station – London Bridge

Goal	Carriage	Door	Side
Exit	3	2/3	R

Direction From – South
Previous Station – Elephant & Castle

Goal	Carriage	Door	Side
Exit	3	3	R

Boston Manor

Piccadilly **No of Carriages = 6**
Direction From – East
Previous Station – Northfields

Goal	Carriage	Door	Side
Exit	6	4	L

Direction From – West
Previous Station – Osterley

Goal	Carriage	Door	Side
Exit	1	2	L

Bounds Green

Piccadilly **No of Carriages = 6**
Direction From – North
Previous Station – Arnos Grove

Goal	Carriage	Door	Side
Exit	4	1	R

Direction From – South
Previous Station – Wood Green

Goal	Carriage	Door	Side
Exit	3	3	R

Bow Road

District **No of Carriages = 6**
Direction From – East
Previous Station – Bromley-by-Bow

Goal	Carriage	Door	Side
DLR	5	4	L
Exit	5	4	L

Bow Road *(cont...)*

District *(cont...)* **No of Carriages = 6**

Direction From – West
Previous Station – Mile End

Goal	Carriage	Door	Side
DLR	1	4	L
Exit	1	4	L

Hammersmith & City **No of Carriages = 6**

Direction From – East
Previous Station – Bromley-by-Bow

Goal	Carriage	Door	Side
Exit	6	3	L
DLR	6	3	L

Direction From – West
Previous Station – Mile End

Goal	Carriage	Door	Side
Exit	1	4	L
DLR	1	4	L

Brent Cross

Northern **No of Carriages = 6**

Direction From – North
Previous Station – Hendon Central

Goal	Carriage	Door	Side
Exit	1	4	R

Direction From – South
Previous Station – Golders Green

Goal	Carriage	Door	Side
Exit	6	1	R

Brixton *(Terminus)*

Victoria **No of Carriages = 8**

Direction From – North
Previous Station – Stockwell

Goal	Carriage	Door	Side
Exit	3	2	L
Exit (Lift)	6	4	L
Rail	3	2	L

Bromley-by-Bow

District **No of Carriages = 6**

Direction From – East
Previous Station – West Ham

Goal	Carriage	Door	Side
Exit	6	2	L

Direction From – West
Previous Station – Bow Road

Goal	Carriage	Door	Side
Exit	1	4	L

Hammersmith & City **No of Carriages = 6**

Direction From – East
Previous Station – West Ham

Goal	Carriage	Door	Side
Exit	6	4	L

Direction From – West
Previous Station – Bow Road

Goal	Carriage	Door	Side
Exit	1	4	L

Buckhurst Hill

Central **No of Carriages = 8**

Direction From – East
Previous Station – Loughton

Goal	Carriage	Door	Side
Exit	8	3	L

Direction From – West
Previous Station – Woodford

Goal	Carriage	Door	Side
Exit	1	2	L

Burnt Oak

Northern **No of Carriages = 6**

Direction From – North
Previous Station – Edgware

Goal	Carriage	Door	Side
Exit	4	3	R
Exit	3	2	R

Direction From – South
Previous Station – Colindale

Goal	Carriage	Door	Side
Exit	3	2	R
Exit	4	3	R

Caledonian Road

Piccadilly **No of Carriages = 6**

Direction From – North East
Previous Station – Holloway Road

Goal	Carriage	Door	Side
Exit	3	3	R

Direction From – South West
Previous Station – King's Cross St. Pancras

Goal	Carriage	Door	Side
Exit	3	4	R

Camden Town

Northern **No of Carriages = 6**

Direction From – North East or North West
Previous Station – Chalk Farm or Kentish Town
Platform 2 (goes South via Bank or Charing X)

Goal	Carriage	Door	Side
Exit	5	1	L
North (Edgware Branch)	5	1	L
South (Bank Branch)	5	1	L
South (Charing Cross Branch)	5	1	L

Direction From – North East or North West
Previous Station – Chalk Farm
Platform 4 (goes South via Bank or Charing X)

Goal	Carriage	Door	Side
Exit	3	3	R
North (Barnet Branch)	3	3	R
South (Bank Branch)	3	3	R
South (Charing Cross Branch)	3	3	R

Direction From – South
Previous Station – Euston or Mornington Crescent
Platform *1 (goes North to Edgware)*

Goal	Carriage	Door	Side
Exit	2	3	R
North (Barnet Branch)	2	3	R
North (Barnet Branch)	5	4	R

Direction From – South
Previous Station – Euston or Mornington Crescent
Platform 3 (goes North to High Barnet/Mill Hill East)

Goal	Carriage	Door	Side
Exit	4	1	L
North (Edgware Branch)	4	1	L

Canada Water

Jubilee **No of Carriages = 7**

Direction From – East
Previous Station – Canary Wharf

Goal	Carriage	Door	Side
Exit	5	4	R
Exit (Stairs)	5	1	R
Lift	3	1	R
Rail	3	1	R

Direction From – West
Previous Station – Bermondsey

Goal	Carriage	Door	Side
Exit	3	1	R
Exit (Stairs)	3	4	R
Lift	5	4	R
Rail	5	4	R

Canary Wharf

Jubilee **No of Carriages = 7**

Direction From – East

Previous Station – North Greenwich

Goal	Carriage	Door	Side
DLR	4	2	R
DLR	2	4	R
DLR	1	2	R
Exit (Upper Bark St)	6	2	R
Exit (Upper Bark St)	7	3	R
Exit	1	2	R
Exit	2	4	R
Exit	4	2	R
Lift	1	1	R

Direction From – West

Previous Station – Canada Water

Goal	Carriage	Door	Side
DLR	6	1	R
DLR	7	2	R
Exit (Upper Bark St)	1	1	R
Exit (Upper Bark St)	2	3	R
Exit	4	3	R
Exit	6	1	R
Exit	7	2	R
Lift	7	3	R

Canning Town

Jubilee **No of Carriages = 7**

Direction From – North

Previous Station – West Ham

Goal	Carriage	Door	Side
DLR	4	2	R
DLR	6	3	R
DLR	5	3	R
Exit	7	2/3	R
Exit (Buses)	2	2	R
Exit (Buses)	5	3	R
Lift	4	2	R
Lift	6	3	R

Direction From – South
Previous Station – North Greenwich

Goal	Carriage	Door	Side
DLR	2	2	R
DLR	3	3	R
DLR	3	4	R
Exit	1	1	R
Exit (Buses)	3	3	R
Exit (Buses)	6	2	R
Lift	2	2	R
Lift	3	4	R

Cannon Street

Circle **No of Carriages = 6**

Direction From – East
Previous Station – Monument

Platform 1

Goal	Carriage	Door	Side
Exit	6	2	L
Rail	6	2	L

Direction From – West
Previous Station – Mansion House

Platform 2

Goal	Carriage	Door	Side
Exit	4	1	L
Rail	4	1	L

Direction From – West *(Terminating)*
Previous Station – Mansion House

Platform 3

Goal	Carriage	Door	Side
Circle & District Eastwards	2	2	R
Exit	2	2	R
Rail	2	2	R

Cannon Street *(cont...)*

District **No of Carriages = 6**

Direction From – East
Previous Station – Monument
Platform 1

Goal	Carriage	Door	Side
Exit	5	2	L
Rail	5	2	L

Direction From – West
Previous Station – Mansion House
Platform 2

Goal	Carriage	Door	Side
Exit	3	3	L
Rail	3	3	L

Canons Park

Jubilee **No of Carriages = 7**

Direction From – North
Previous Station – Stanmore

Goal	Carriage	Door	Side
Exit	1	4	L

Direction From – South
Previous Station – Queensbury

Goal	Carriage	Door	Side
Exit	7	1	L

Chalk Farm

Northern **No of Carriages = 6**

Direction From – North
Previous Station – Belsize Park

Goal	Carriage	Door	Side
Exit	6	4	R

Direction From – South
Previous Station – Camden Town

Goal	Carriage	Door	Side
Exit	1	1	R

Chalfont & Latimer

Metropolitan

No of Carriages = 8

Direction From – East
Previous Station – Chorley Wood
Platform 1

Goal	Carriage	Door	Side
Exit	6	1	L
Rail (to Amersham)	Any	Any	L
Rail (to London)	6	1	L
Metropolitan (To Chesham)	6	1	L

Direction From – West
Previous Station – Amersham
Platform 2

Goal	Carriage	Door	Side
Exit	3	3	L
Metropolitan (To Chesham)	5 - 8	Any	L

Direction From – West
Previous Station – Chesham
Platform 3 *(Terminus)*

Goal	Carriage	Door	Side
Exit	1	1	R
Metropolitan (To Amersham)	1	1	R
Rail (to Amersham)	1	1	R
Rail (to London)	Any	Any	R

Chancery Lane

Central

No of Carriages = 8

Direction From – East
Previous Station – St Paul's

Goal	Carriage	Door	Side
Exit	6	2	R

Direction From – West
Previous Station – Holborn

Goal	Carriage	Door	Side
Exit	1	1	L

Charing Cross

Bakerloo **No of Carriages = 7**

Direction From – North
Previous Station – Piccadilly Circus

Goal	Carriage	Door	Side
Exit	1	1	R
Northern	1	1	R
Rail	1	1	R

Direction From – South
Previous Station – Embankment

Goal	Carriage	Door	Side
Exit	7	3	R
Northern	7	3	R
Rail	7	3	R

Northern **No of Carriages = 6**

Direction From – North
Previous Station – Leicester Square

Goal	Carriage	Door	Side
Bakerloo	2	4	R
Exit	2	4	R
Rail	2	4	R

Direction From – South
Previous Station – Embankment

Goal	Carriage	Door	Side
Bakerloo	4	3	R
Exit	4	3	R
Rail	4	3	R

Chesham *(Terminus)*

Metropolitan **No of Carriages = 8**

Direction From –East (Terminal)
Previous Station – Chalfont & Latimer

Goal	Carriage	Door	Side
Exit	2	1	L

Chigwell

Central **No of Carriages = 8**

Direction From – West
Previous Station – Roding Valley

Goal	Carriage	Door	Side
Exit	8	3	L

Direction From – South
Previous Station – Grange Hill

Goal	Carriage	Door	Side
Exit	1	1	L

Chiswick Park

District **No of Carriages = 6**

Direction From – East
Previous Station – Turnham Green

Goal	Carriage	Door	Side
Exit	5	3	L

Direction From – West
Previous Station – Acton Town

Goal	Carriage	Door	Side
Exit	3	4	L

Chorleywood

Metropolitan **No of Carriages = 8**

Direction From – West
Previous Station – Chalfont & Latimer

Goal	Carriage	Door	Side
Exit	7	3	L

Direction From – South East
Previous Station – Rickmansworth

Goal	Carriage	Door	Side
Exit	3	3	L

Clapham Common

Northern — **No of Carriages = 6**

Direction From – North
Previous Station – Clapham North

Goal	Carriage	Door	Side
Exit	1	1	R

Direction From – South
Previous Station – Clapham South

Goal	Carriage	Door	Side
Exit	6	4	R

Clapham North

Northern — **No of Carriages = 6**

Direction From – North
Previous Station – Stockwell

Goal	Carriage	Door	Side
Exit	1	1	R

Direction From – South
Previous Station – Clapham Common

Goal	Carriage	Door	Side
Exit	6	4	R

Clapham South

Northern — **No of Carriages = 6**

Direction From – North
Previous Station – Clapham Common

Goal	Carriage	Door	Side
Exit	1	1	R

Direction From – South
Previous Station – Balham

Goal	Carriage	Door	Side
Exit	6	4	R

Cockfosters *(Terminus)*

Piccadilly — **No of Carriages = 6**

Direction From – South (Terminal)
Previous Station – Oakwood

Goal	Carriage	Door	Side
Exit	1	1	R

Colindale

Northern **No of Carriages = 6**

Direction From – North
Previous Station – Burnt Oak

Goal	Carriage	Door	Side
Exit	5	1	R

Direction From – South
Previous Station – Hendon Central

Goal	Carriage	Door	Side
Exit	2	4	R

Colliers Wood

Northern **No of Carriages = 6**

Direction From – North
Previous Station – Tooting Broadway

Goal	Carriage	Door	Side
Exit	3	4	R

Direction From – South
Previous Station – South Wimbledon

Goal	Carriage	Door	Side
Exit	4	1	R

Covent Garden

Piccadilly **No of Carriages = 6**

Direction From – North East
Previous Station – Holborn

Goal	Carriage	Door	Side
Exit	5	3	R

Direction From – South West
Previous Station – Leicester Square

Goal	Carriage	Door	Side
Exit	2	3	R

Croxley

Metropolitan **No of Carriages = 8**

Direction From – North
Previous Station – Watford

Goal	Carriage	Door	Side
Exit	2	1	L

Direction From – South East
Previous Station – Moor Park

Goal	Carriage	Door	Side
Exit	7	3	L

Dagenham East

District **No of Carriages = 6**

Direction From – North East
Previous Station – Elm Park

Goal	Carriage	Door	Side
Exit	6	4	L

Direction From – South West
Previous Station – Dagenham Heathway

Goal	Carriage	Door	Side
Exit	1	1	L

Dagenham Heathway

District **No of Carriages = 6**

Direction From – North East
Previous Station – Dagenham East

Goal	Carriage	Door	Side
Exit	6	4	R

Direction From – South West
Previous Station – Becontree

Goal	Carriage	Door	Side
Exit	1	1	R

Debden

Central **No of Carriages = 8**

Direction From – North East
Previous Station – Theydon Bois

Goal	Carriage	Door	Side
Exit	3	2	L

Direction From – South West
Previous Station – Loughton

Goal	Carriage	Door	Side
Exit	5	2	L

Dollis Hill

Jubilee **No of Carriages = 7**

Direction From – North
Previous Station – Neasden

Goal	Carriage	Door	Side
Exit	3	3	R

Direction From – South
Previous Station – Willesden Green

Goal	Carriage	Door	Side
Exit	5	2	R

Ealing Broadway *(Terminus)*

Central **No of Carriages = 8**

Direction From – East
Previous Station – West Acton

Goal	Carriage	Door	Side
District	1	1	L/R
Exit	1	1	L/R
Rail	1	1	L/R

Ealing Broadway *(cont...)*

District *(Terminus)*

Direction From – South
Previous Station – Ealing Common

If arriving at Platform 7

Goal	Carriage	Door	Side
Central	1	3	R
Exit	1	3	R
Rail	1	3	R

Direction From – South
Previous Station – Ealing Common

If arriving at Platform 8

Goal	Carriage	Door	Side
Central	1	1	L
Exit	1	1	L
Rail	1	1	L

Ealing Common

District **No of Carriages = 6**

Direction From – North
Previous Station – Ealing Broadway

Goal	Carriage	Door	Side
Exit	5	4	L
Piccadilly North-Bound	5	4	L
Piccadilly South-Bound	Any	Any	L

Direction From – South
Previous Station – Acton Town

Goal	Carriage	Door	Side
Exit	1	4	L
Piccadilly North-Bound	Any	Any	L

Piccadilly **No of Carriages = 6**

Direction From – North
Previous Station – North Ealing

Goal	Carriage	Door	Side
District (to Ealing Broadway)	6	1	L
Exit	6	1	L

Direction From – South
Previous Station – Acton Town

Goal	Carriage	Door	Side
Exit	1	4	L

Earl's Court

District **No of Carriages = 6**

Direction From – East
Previous Station – Gloucester Road/High Street Kensington
Platform 3

Goal	Carriage	Door	Side
Exit (Earls Court Exhibition)	5	4	L
Exit (Warwick Road)	1	1	L
Lift	3	3	L
Piccadilly	3	1	L

Direction From – East
Previous Station – Notting Hill Gate/Gloucester Road
Platform 4

Goal	Carriage	Door	Side
Exit (Earls Court Exhibition)	5	4	R
Exit (Warwick Road)	1	1	R
Lift	3	2	R
Piccadilly	3	4	R

Direction From – West/Left
Previous Station – Olympia/West Brompton/West Kensington
If arriving at Platform 1

Goal	Carriage	Door	Side
Exit (Earls Court Exhibition)	1	1	R
Exit (Warwick Road)	6	3	R
Lift	4	1	R
Piccadilly	3	4	R

If arriving at Platform 2

Goal	Carriage	Door	Side
Exit (Earls Court Exhibition)	1	2	L
Exit (Warwick Road)	6	4	L
Lift	4	4	L
Piccadilly	6	2	L

Earl's Court *(cont...)*

Piccadilly **No of Carriages = 6**

Direction From – East
Previous Station – Gloucester Road

Goal	Carriage	Door	Side
Exit Warwick Rd and Exhibition	2	2/3	R
District	2	2/3	R
Exit Lift	3	4	R
Exit (Earls Court Rd)	3	4	R

Direction From – West
Previous Station – Barons Court

Goal	Carriage	Door	Side
Exit Warwick Rd and Exhibition	5	1	R
District	5	1	R
Exit Lift	3	3	R
Exit	5	1	R

East Acton

Central **No of Carriages = 8**

Direction From – East
Previous Station – White City

Goal	Carriage	Door	Side
Exit	8	3	L

Direction From – West
Previous Station – North Acton

Goal	Carriage	Door	Side
Exit	1	1	L

East Finchley

Northern **No of Carriages = 6**

Direction From – North
Previous Station – Finchley Central

Goal	Carriage	Door	Side
Exit	2	2	L/R

Direction From – South
Previous Station – Highgate

Goal	Carriage	Door	Side
Exit	5	2	L/R

East Ham

District — **No of Carriages = 6**

Direction From – East
Previous Station – Barking

Goal	Carriage	Door	Side
Exit	1	1	L
Lift	1	1	L

Direction From – West
Previous Station – Upton Park

Goal	Carriage	Door	Side
Exit	6	4	L
Lift	6	3	L

Hammersmith & City — **No of Carriages = 6**

Direction From – East
Previous Station – Barking

Goal	Carriage	Door	Side
Exit	1	1	L
Lift	1	1	L

Direction From – West
Previous Station – Upton Park

Goal	Carriage	Door	Side
Exit	6	4	L
Lift	6	4	L

East Putney

District — **No of Carriages = 6**

Direction From – North
Previous Station – Putney Bridge

Goal	Carriage	Door	Side
Exit	5	1	L

Direction From – South
Previous Station – South Fields

Goal	Carriage	Door	Side
Exit	3	2	L

Eastcote

Metropolitan **No of Carriages = 8**

Direction From – East
Previous Station – Rayners Lane

Goal	Carriage	Door	Side
Exit	1	2	L

Direction From – West
Previous Station – Ruislip Manor

Goal	Carriage	Door	Side
Exit	8	1	L

Piccadilly **No of Carriages = 6**

Direction From – East
Previous Station – Rayners Lane

Goal	Carriage	Door	Side
Exit	1	2	L

Direction From – West
Previous Station – Ruislip Manor

Goal	Carriage	Door	Side
Exit	6	3	L

Edgware *(Terminus)*

Northern **No of Carriages = 6**

Direction From – South
Previous Station – Burnt Oak

Depending on arrival platform

Goal	Carriage	Door	Side
Exit	1	4	L/R
Exit	3	3	L/R

Edgware Road (Annexe)

Bakerloo **No of Carriages = 7**

Direction From – East
Previous Station – Marylebone

Goal	Carriage	Door	Side
District & Circle	5	3	L
East London	5	3	L
Exit	5	3	L
Hammersmith & City	5	3	L

Direction From – West
Previous Station – Paddington

Goal	Carriage	Door	Side
District & Circle	4	1	L
East London	4	1	L
Exit	4	1	L
Hammersmith & City	4	1	L

Edgware Road (Main)

Circle **No of Carriages = 6**

Direction From – East
Previous Station – Baker Street

Goal	Carriage	Door	Side
Bakerloo	1	1	R
Circle (towards Victoria)	3	3	R
Circle (towards Victoria)	5	2	R
District	Any	Any	R
Exit	1	1	R

Direction From – West *(Terminus)*
Previous Station – Paddington/Bayswater

Goal	Carriage	Door	Side
Bakerloo	6	4	R
Circle (Eastwards)	Any	Any	R
District	2	2	R
District	3	4	R
Exit	6	4	R
Ham. & City Eastwards	Any	Any	R

Direction From – West
Previous Station – Paddington/Royal Oak

Goal	Carriage	Door	Side
Bakerloo	6	4	L
District	2	2	L
District	3	4	L
Exit	6	4	L

Edgware Road *(cont...)*

District *(Terminus)* **No of Carriages = 6**

Direction From – West

Previous Station – Paddington

Goal	Carriage	Door	Side
Exit	6	4	R
Bakerloo	6	4	R
Circle towards Hammersmith	Any	Any	R
Circle East	2	2	R
Circle East	4	1	R
Hammersmith & City East	2	2	R
Hammersmith & City East	4	1	R

Hammersmith & City **No of Carriages = 6**

Direction From – East

Previous Station – Baker Street

Goal	Carriage	Door	Side
Bakerloo	1	1	R
Circle	3	3	R
Circle	5	2	R
District	Any	Any	R
Exit	1	1	R

Direction From – West

Previous Station – Paddington

Goal	Carriage	Door	Side
Bakerloo	6	4	L
Circle (towards Victoria)	2	1	L
Circle (towards Victoria)	3	4	L
District	2	1	L
District	3	4	L
Exit	6	4	L

Elephant Castle

Bakerloo *(Terminus)* **No of Carriages = 7**

Direction From – North

Previous Station – Lambeth North

Goal	Carriage	Door	Side
Exit	6	3	L/R
Northern	6	3	L/R

Northern **No of Carriages = 6**

Direction From – North
Previous Station – Borough

Goal	Carriage	Door	Side
Bakerloo	6	3/4	L
Exit (South Bank University)	6	3/4	L
Exit (Shopping Centre)	3	1/2	L
Rail	3	1/2	L

Direction From – South
Previous Station – Kennington

Goal	Carriage	Door	Side
Bakerloo	1	1	L
Exit (South Bank University)	1	1	L
Exit (Shopping Centre)	5	3	L
Rail	5	3	L

Elm Park

District **No of Carriages = 6**

Direction From – East
Previous Station – Hornchurch

Goal	Carriage	Door	Side
Exit	6	4	R

Direction From – West
Previous Station – Dagenham East

Goal	Carriage	Door	Side
Exit	1	1	R

Embankment

Bakerloo **No of Carriages = 7**

Direction From – North
Previous Station – Charing Cross

Goal	Carriage	Door	Side
District & Circle	3	2	L
Exit	3	2	L
Northern	3	2	L
River Boat	3	2	L

Embankment *(cont...)*

Bakerloo *(cont...)* **No of Carriages = 7**

Direction From – South
Previous Station – Waterloo

Goal	Carriage	Door	Side
District & Circle	5	2	L
Exit	5	2	L
Northern	5	2	L
River Boat	5	2	L

Circle **No of Carriages = 6**

Direction From – East
Previous Station – Temple

Goal	Carriage	Door	Side
Bakerloo	4	3	L
Exit	4	3	L
Northern	4	3	L
Rail	4	3	L

Direction From – West
Previous Station – Westminster

Goal	Carriage	Door	Side
Bakerloo	6	4	L
Exit	6	2	L
Northern	6	4	L
Rail	6	2	L

District **No of Carriages = 6**

Direction From – East
Previous Station – Temple

Goal	Carriage	Door	Side
Bakerloo	4	1	L
Exit	4	1	L
Northern	4	1	L
Rail	4	1	L

Direction From – West
Previous Station – Westminster

Goal	Carriage	Door	Side
Bakerloo	5	3	L
Exit	5	4	L
Northern	5	3	L
Rail	5	4	L

Northern **No of Carriages = 6**

Direction From – North
Previous Station – Charing Cross

Goal	Carriage	Door	Side
Bakerloo	3	4	R
Circle	3	4	R
District	3	4	R
Exit	3	4	R
Rail	3	4	R
River Boat	3	4	R

Direction From – South
Previous Station – Waterloo

Goal	Carriage	Door	Side
Bakerloo	4	1/2	R
Circle	4	1/2	R
District	4	1/2	R
Exit	4	1/2	R
Rail	4	1/2	R
River Boat	4	1/2	R

Epping *(Terminus)*

Central **No of Carriages = 8**

Direction From – South
Previous Station – Theydon Bois

Goal	Carriage	Door	Side
Exit (via Footbridge)	2	3	R
Exit	4	3	L

Euston

Northern Bank Branch — No of Carriages = 6

Direction From – North
Previous Station – Camden Town

Goal	Carriage	Door	Side
Exit	4	2	R
Northern (Charing Cross Branch)	4	2	R
Rail	4	2	R
Victoria (North-Bound)	4	2	R
Victoria (South-Bound)	6	4	R
Victoria (South-Bound)	5	1	R
Victoria (South-Bound)	4	2	R
Victoria (South-Bound)	3	3	R
Victoria (South-Bound)	1	4	R

Direction From – South
Previous Station – King's Cross St. Pancras

Goal	Carriage	Door	Side
Exit	2	3/4	R
Northern (Charing Cross Branch)	2	3/4	R
Rail	2	3/4	R
Victoria (North-Bound)	1	1	R
Victoria (North-Bound)	3	3	R
Victoria (North-Bound)	6	4	R
Victoria (South-Bound)	2	3/4	R

Northern Charing X Branch — No of Carriages = 6

Direction From – North
Previous Station – Mornington Crescent

Goal	Carriage	Door	Side
Exit	6	3	R
Northern (Bank Branch)	6	3	R
Rail	6	3	R
Victoria	6	3	R

Direction From – South
Previous Station – Warren Street

Goal	Carriage	Door	Side
Exit	1	1	R
Northern (Bank Branch)	1	1	R
Rail	1	1	R
Victoria	1	1	R

Victoria **No of Carriages = 8**

Direction From – North
Previous Station – King's Cross St. Pancras

Goal	Carriage	Door	Side
Exit	2	4	R
Northern (Bank Branch N'Bound)	2	4	R
Northern (Bank Branch S'Bound)	2	4	R
Northern (Bank Branch S'Bound)	4	2	R
Northern (Bank Branch S'Bound)	5	4	R
Northern (Charing Cross Branch)	2	4	R
Rail	2	4	R

Direction From – South
Previous Station – Warren Street

Goal	Carriage	Door	Side
Exit	6	3	R
Northern Bank Branch N'Bound	2	4	R
Northern Bank Branch N'Bound	3	1	R
Northern Bank Branch N'Bound	8	3	R
Northern Bank Branch S'Bound	8	3	R
Northern (Charing Cross Branch)	6	3	R
Rail	6	3	R

Euston Square

Circle **No of Carriages = 6**

Direction From – East
Previous Station – King's Cross St. Pancras

Goal	Carriage	Door	Side
Exit	1	4	L
Hammersmith & City	Any	Any	L
Metropolitan	Any	Any	L

Euston Square *(cont...)*

Circle *(cont...)* **No of Carriages = 6**

Direction From – West
Previous Station – Great Portland Street

Goal	Carriage	Door	Side
Exit	6	1	L
Hammersmith & City	Any	Any	L
Metropolitan	Any	Any	L

Hammersmith & City **No of Carriages = 6**

Direction From – East
Previous Station – King's Cross St. Pancras

Goal	Carriage	Door	Side
Exit	1	4	L
Circle	Any	Any	L
Metropolitan	Any	Any	L

Direction From – West
Previous Station – Great Portland Street

Goal	Carriage	Door	Side
Exit	6	1	L
Circle	Any	Any	L
Metropolitan	Any	Any	L

Metropolitan **No of Carriages = 8**

Direction From – East
Previous Station – King's Cross St. Pancras

Goal	Carriage	Door	Side
Exit	1	2	L
Circle	Any	Any	L
Hammersmith & City	Any	Any	L

Direction From – West
Previous Station – Great Portland Street

Goal	Carriage	Door	Side
Exit	7	2	L
Circle	Any	Any	L
Hammersmith & City	Any	Any	L

Fairlop

Central **No of Carriages = 8**

Direction From – North
Previous Station – Hainault

Goal	Carriage	Door	Side
Exit	1	2	L

Direction From – South
Previous Station – Barkingside

Goal	Carriage	Door	Side
Exit	8	3	L

Farringdon

Circle **No of Carriages = 6**

Direction From – East
Previous Station – Barbican

Goal	Carriage	Door	Side
Exit	6	4	L
Hammersmith & City	Any	Any	L
Metropolitan	Any	Any	L
Rail North-Bound)	3	2	L
Rail South-Bound)	4	1	L
Rail South-Bound)	6	1	L

Direction From – West
Previous Station – King's Cross St. Pancras

Goal	Carriage	Door	Side
Exit	2	3	L
Hammersmith & City	Any	Any	L
Metropolitan	Any	Any	L
Rail (North-Bound)	2	3	L
Rail (South-Bound)	2	3	L

Farringdon *(cont...)*

Hammersmith & City **No of Carriages = 6**

Direction From – East
Previous Station – Barbican

Goal	Carriage	Door	Side
Circle	Any	Any	L
Exit	6	4	L
Metropolitan	Any	Any	L
Rail (North-Bound)	3	2	L
Rail (South-Bound)	4	1	L
Rail (South-Bound)	6	1	L

Direction From – West
Previous Station – King's Cross St. Pancras

Goal	Carriage	Door	Side
Circle	Any	Any	L
Exit	6	6	L
Metropolitan	Any	Any	L
Rail (North-Bound)	2	3	L
Rail (South-Bound)	2	3	L

Metropolitan **No of Carriages = 8**

Direction From – East
Previous Station – Barbican

Goal	Carriage	Door	Side
Circle	Any	Any	L
Exit	6	4	L
Hammersmith & City	Any	Any	L
Rail (North-Bound)	3	2	L
Rail (South-Bound)	4	1	L
Rail (South-Bound)	6	1	L

Direction From – West
Previous Station – King's Cross St. Pancras

Goal	Carriage	Door	Side
Circle	Any	Any	L
Exit	6	6	L
Metropolitan	Any	Any	L
Rail (North-Bound)	2	3	L
Rail (South-Bound)	2	3	L

Finchley Central

Northern — **No of Carriages = 6**

Direction From – North West
Previous Station – Mill Hill East

Goal	Carriage	Door	Side
Exit	4	2	L

Direction From – North
Previous Station – West Finchley

Goal	Carriage	Door	Side
Exit	4	4	L
Lift	5	1	L

Direction From – South
Previous Station – East Finchley

Goal	Carriage	Door	Side
Exit & Lift	3	2	L/R

Finchley Road

Jubilee — **No of Carriages = 7**

Direction From – North
Previous Station – West Hampstead

Goal	Carriage	Door	Side
Exit	1	1/2	L
Metropolitan	Any	Any	L

Direction From – South
Previous Station – Swiss Cottage

Goal	Carriage	Door	Side
Exit	7	3	L
Metropolitan	Any	Any	L

Metropolitan — **No of Carriages = 8**

Direction From – North
Previous Station – Wembley Park

Goal	Carriage	Door	Side
Exit	1	1	R
Jubilee	Any	Any	R

Finchley Road *(cont...)*

Metropolitan *(cont...)* **No of Carriages = 8**

Direction From – South
Previous Station – Baker Street

Goal	Carriage	Door	Side
Exit	8	3	R
Jubilee	Any	Any	R

Finsbury Park

Piccadilly **No of Carriages = 6**

Direction From – North
Previous Station – Manor House

Goal	Carriage	Door	Side
Exit	1	2	L
Exit	4	3	L
Rail	4	3	L
Victoria North	1	2	L
Victoria North	4	3	L
Victoria South	1	2	L
Victoria South	2	3	L
Victoria South	4	3	L
Victoria South	5	3	L
Victoria South	6	2	L

Direction From – South
Previous Station – Arsenal

Goal	Carriage	Door	Side
Exit	3	3	R
Exit	6	2	R
Rail	3	3	R
Victoria North	1	3	R
Victoria North	2	3	R
Victoria North	3	2	R
Victoria North	3	3	R
Victoria North	6	2	R
Victoria South	3	3	R
Victoria South	5	3/2	R
Victoria South	6	2	R

Victoria **No of Carriages = 8**

Direction From – North
Previous Station – Seven Sisters

Goal	Carriage	Door	Side
Exit	2	1	R
Exit	5	1	R
Piccadilly North	2	1	R
Piccadilly North	5	1	R
Piccadilly South	2	1	R
Piccadilly South	3	1	R
Piccadilly South	5	1/3	R
Piccadilly South	6	4	R
Rail	5	1	R

Direction From – South
Previous Station – Highbury & Islington

Goal	Carriage	Door	Side
Exit	8	1	L
Exit	5	1	L
Piccadilly North	8	1	L
Piccadilly North	7	2	L
Piccadilly North	3	2	L
Piccadilly North	4	1/4	L
Piccadilly North	3	2	L
Piccadilly South	8	1	L
Piccadilly South	5	1	L
Rail	5	1	L

Fulham Broadway

District **No of Carriages = 6**

Direction From – North
Previous Station – West Brompton

Goal	Carriage	Door	Side
Exit	5	2	L
Lift	6	1	L

Direction From – South
Previous Station – Parsons Green

Goal	Carriage	Door	Side
Exit	3	3	L
Lift	2	2	L

Gants Hill

Central **No of Carriages = 8**

Direction From – East

Previous Station – Newbury Park

Goal	Carriage	Door	Side
Exit	8	2	R

Direction From – West

Previous Station – Redbridge

Goal	Carriage	Door	Side
Exit	1	2	R

Gloucester Road

Circle **No of Carriages = 6**

Direction From – East

Previous Station – South Kensington

Goal	Carriage	Door	Side
District (West-Bound)	5	3	R
Exit	5	3	R
Piccadilly	5	3	R

Direction From – North

Previous Station – High Street Kensington

Goal	Carriage	Door	Side
District (West-Bound)	3	2	R
Exit	3	2	R
Piccadilly	3	2	R

District **No of Carriages = 6**

Direction From – East

Previous Station – South Kensington

Goal	Carriage	Door	Side
Circle (towards Paddington)	5	4	L
Exit	5	4	L
Piccadilly	5	4	L

Direction From – West

Previous Station – Earl's Court

Goal	Carriage	Door	Side
Circle (towards Paddington)	Any	Any	R
Exit	3	3	R
Piccadilly	3	3	R

Piccadilly **No of Carriages = 6**

Direction From – East
Previous Station – South Kensington

Goal	Carriage	Door	Side
Circle	6	3	R
District	6	3	R
Exit	6	3	R

Direction From – West
Previous Station – Earl's Court

Goal	Carriage	Door	Side
Circle	1	2	R
District	1	2	R
Exit	1	2	R

Golders Green

Northern **No of Carriages = 6**

Direction From – North
Previous Station – Brent Cross

Goal	Carriage	Door	Side
Exit	4	3	L/R

Direction From – South
Previous Station – Hampstead

Goal	Carriage	Door	Side
Exit	3	2	L/R

Goldhawk Road

Circle **No of Carriages = 6**

Direction From – North
Previous Station – Shepherd's Bush Market

Goal	Carriage	Door	Side
Exit	6	4	L
Hammersmith & City	Any	Any	L

Direction From – South
Previous Station – Hammersmith

Goal	Carriage	Door	Side
Exit	1	1	L
Hammersmith & City	Any	Any	L

Goldhawk Road *(cont...)*

Hammersmith & City **No of Carriages = 6**

Direction From – North
Previous Station – Shepherd's Bush Market

Goal	Carriage	Door	Side
Circle	Any	Any	L
Exit	6	4	L

Direction From – South
Previous Station – Hammersmith

Goal	Carriage	Door	Side
Circle	Any	Any	L
Exit	1	1	L

Goodge Street

Northern **No of Carriages = 6**

Direction From – North
Previous Station – Warren Street

Goal	Carriage	Door	Side
Exit	4	2	R

Direction From – South
Previous Station – Tottenham Court Road

Goal	Carriage	Door	Side
Exit	3	2	R

Grange Hill

Central **No of Carriages = 8**

Direction From – North
Previous Station – Chigwell

Goal	Carriage	Door	Side
Exit	8	3	L

Direction From – South
Previous Station – Hainault

Goal	Carriage	Door	Side
Exit	1	1	L

Great Portland Street

Circle **No of Carriages = 6**

Direction From – East
Previous Station – Euston Square

Goal	Carriage	Door	Side
Exit	2	4	L
Exit	3	4	L
Hammersmith & City	Any	Any	L
Metropolitan	Any	Any	L

Direction From – West
Previous Station – Baker Street

Goal	Carriage	Door	Side
Exit	6	4	L
Hammersmith & City	Any	Any	L
Metropolitan	Any	Any	L

Hammersmith & City **No of Carriages = 6**

Direction From – East
Previous Station – Euston Square

Goal	Carriage	Door	Side
Circle	Any	Any	L
Exit	2	4	L
Exit	3	4	L
Metropolitan	Any	Any	L

Direction From – West
Previous Station – Baker Street

Goal	Carriage	Door	Side
Circle	Any	Any	L
Exit	6	4	L
Metropolitan	Any	Any	L

Metropolitan **No of Carriages = 8**

Direction From – East
Previous Station – Euston Square

Goal	Carriage	Door	Side
Circle	Any	Any	L
Exit	2	3	L
Hammersmith & City	Any	Any	L

Great Portland Street *(cont...)*

Metropolitan *(cont...)* **No of Carriages = 6**

Direction From – West

Previous Station – Baker Street

Goal	Carriage	Door	Side
Circle	Any	Any	L
Exit	6	2	L
Hammersmith & City	Any	Any	L

Green Park

Jubilee **No of Carriages = 7**

Direction From – North

Previous Station – Bond Street

Goal	Carriage	Door	Side
Exit	4	3	R
Piccadilly	2	3	R
Victoria	4	3	R

Direction From – South

Previous Station – Westminster

Goal	Carriage	Door	Side
Exit	2	4	R
Piccadilly	6	2	R
Victoria	2	4	R

Piccadilly **No of Carriages = 6**

Direction From – East

Previous Station – Piccadilly Circus

Goal	Carriage	Door	Side
Exit	1	1	R
Jubilee	3	1	R
Victoria	2	3	R

Direction From – West

Previous Station – Hyde Park Corner

Goal	Carriage	Door	Side
Exit	6	4	R
Jubilee	4	3	R
Victoria	5	3	R

Victoria **No of Carriages = 8**

Direction From – North
Previous Station – Oxford Circus

Goal	Carriage	Door	Side
Exit	5	1	R
Lift	8	3	R
Jubilee	1	3	R
Piccadilly	7	3	R

Direction From – South
Previous Station – Victoria

Goal	Carriage	Door	Side
Exit	4	1	R
Lift	1	1	R
Jubilee	8	3	R
Piccadilly	4	1	R

Greenford

Central **No of Carriages = 8**

Direction From – North
Previous Station – Northolt

Goal	Carriage	Door	Side
Exit	8	3	R
Rail	1-5	Any	R

Direction From – South
Previous Station – Perivale

Goal	Carriage	Door	Side
Exit	1	1	R
Rail	3-8	Any	R

Gunnersbury

District **No of Carriages = 6**

Direction From – North
Previous Station – Turnham Green

Goal	Carriage	Door	Side
Exit	6	4	R

Direction From – South
Previous Station – Kew Gardens

Goal	Carriage	Door	Side
Exit	1	1	R

Hainault

Central **No of Carriages = 8**

Direction From – North
Previous Station – Grange Hill

Goal	Carriage	Door	Side
Exit (via Footbridge)	8	3	L

Direction From – South
Previous Station – Fairlop

Goal	Carriage	Door	Side
Exit	1	2	L/R

Hammersmith

Circle *(Terminus)* **No of Carriages = 6**

Direction From – North
Previous Station – Goldhawk Road

Goal	Carriage	Door	Side
District	1	1	L/R
Exit	1	1	L/R
Hammersmith & City	1	1	L/R
Lift	1	1	L/R
Piccadilly	1	1	L/R

District **No of Carriages = 6**

Direction From – East
Previous Station – Barons Court

Goal	Carriage	Door	Side
Circle	2	2	R
Exit	2	2	R
Exit (Talgarth Rd & Buses)	4	3	R
Hammersmith & City	2	2	R
Lift	1	1	R
Piccadilly	Any	Any	R

Direction From – West
Previous Station – Ravenscourt Park

Goal	Carriage	Door	Side
Circle	5	4	R
Exit	5	4	R
Exit (Talgarth Rd & Buses)	2	4	R
Hammersmith & City	5	4	R
Lift	6	2	R
Piccadilly	Any	Any	R

Hammersmith & City *(Terminus)* **No of Carriages = 6**
Direction From – North
Previous Station – Goldhawk Road

Goal	Carriage	Door	Side
Circle	1	1	L/R
Exit	1	1	L/R
Piccadilly	1	1	L/R
District	1	1	L/R

Piccadilly **No of Carriages = 6**
Direction From – East
Previous Station – Barons Court

Goal	Carriage	Door	Side
Exit (Talgarth Rd & Buses)	5	4	L
Lift	1	1	L
Exit	2	3	L
Hammersmith & City	2	3	L

Direction From – West
Previous Station – Turnham Green

Goal	Carriage	Door	Side
Exit (Talgarth Rd & Buses)	3	1	L
Lift	6	3	L
Exit	5	3	L
Hammersmith & City	5	3	L

Hampstead

Northern — **No of Carriages = 6**

Direction From – North
Previous Station – Golders Green

Goal	Carriage	Door	Side
Exit	3	2	R

Direction From – South
Previous Station – Belsize Park

Goal	Carriage	Door	Side
Exit	4	2	R

Hanger Lane

Central — **No of Carriages = 8**

Direction From – North
Previous Station – Perivale

Goal	Carriage	Door	Side
Exit	1	2	R

Direction From – South
Previous Station – North Acton

Goal	Carriage	Door	Side
Exit	8	2	R

Harlesden

Bakerloo — **No of Carriages = 7**

Direction From – North
Previous Station – Stonebridge Park

Goal	Carriage	Door	Side
Exit	1	1	L

Direction From – South
Previous Station – Willesden Junction

Goal	Carriage	Door	Side
Exit	7	3	L

Harrow & Wealdstone *(Terminus)*

Bakerloo **No of Carriages = 7**

Direction From – South
Previous Station – South Kenton

Goal	Carriage	Door	Side
Exit (Wealdstone)	2	1	L
Rail	2	1	L
Lift	2	1	L
Exit (Harrow)	3	2	L
Exit (Harrow)	4	2	L

Harrow-on-the-Hill

Metropolitan **No of Carriages = 8**

Direction From – East
Previous Station – Northwick Park

Goal	Carriage	Door	Side
Exit	2	2	L/R
Rail	2	2	L/R
Rail	3	2	L/R

Direction From – West
Previous Station – North Harrow/West Harrow

Goal	Carriage	Door	Side
Exit	7	1	L/R
Metropolitan North/Westwards	7	1	L/R
Rail	6	1	L/R
Rail	7	1	L/R

Hatton Cross

Piccadilly **No of Carriages = 6**

Direction From – East
Previous Station – Hounslow West

Goal	Carriage	Door	Side
Exit	4	4	R
Exit	6	3	R

Direction From – West
Previous Station – Heathrow

Goal	Carriage	Door	Side
Exit	2	4	R
Exit	1	3	R

Heathrow Terminal 4

Piccadilly **No of Carriages = 6**

Direction From – East

Previous Station – Hatton Cross

Goal	Carriage	Door	Side
Exit	2	4	R
Exit Lift	2	4	R

Heathrow Terminal 5

Piccadilly **No of Carriages = 6**

Direction From – East

Previous Station – Heathrow Terminals 1,2,3

Goal	Carriage	Door	Side
Exit	1	1	R
Exit Lift	1	1	R

Heathrow Terminals 1,2,3

Piccadilly **No of Carriages = 6**

Direction From – East

Previous Station – Hatton Cross

Goal	Carriage	Door	Side
Exit	3	3	R

Direction From – West

Previous Station – Heathrow Terminal 4/5

Goal	Carriage	Door	Side
Exit Lift	4	2	R

Hendon Central

Northern **No of Carriages = 6**

Direction From – North

Previous Station – Colindale

Goal	Carriage	Door	Side
Exit	4	2	R

Direction From – South

Previous Station – Brent Cross

Goal	Carriage	Door	Side
Exit	3	2	R

High Barnet *(Terminus)*

Northern **No of Carriages = 6**

Direction From – South
Previous Station – Totteridge & Whetstone

Exit depends on platform arrived at..

Goal	Carriage	Door	Side
Exit or	3	3	L/R
Exit	1	2	L/R

High Street Kensington

District & Circle **N**

Direction From – North
Previous Station – Gloucester Road/Notting Hill Gate

Goal	Carriage	Door	Side
Exit	5	3	L

Direction From – South
Previous Station – Gloucester Road

Goal	Carriage	Door	Side
Exit	4	3	L

Highbury & Islington

Victoria **No of Carriages = 8**

Direction From – North
Previous Station – Finsbury Park

Goal	Carriage	Door	Side
Exit	1	3/4	L
Rail Moorgate	6	2	L
Rail Moorgate	4	3	L
Rail Moorgate	3	1	L
Rail Moorgate	1	3/4	L
Rail Richmond & Stratford Line	1	3/4	L
Rail W G City & Hertford	1	3/4	L

Highbury & Islington *(cont...)*

Victoria *(cont...)* **No of Carriages = 6**

Direction From – South

Previous Station – King's Cross St. Pancras

Goal	Carriage	Door	Side
Exit	8	2	R
Rail Moorgate	8	2	R
Rail Richmond & Stratford Line	8	2	R
Rail W G City & Hertford	1	3	R
Rail W G City & Hertford	3	3	R
Rail W G City & Hertford	5	3	R

Highgate

Northern **No of Carriages = 6**

Direction From – North

Previous Station – East Finchley

Goal	Carriage	Door	Side
Exit	4	2	R

Direction From – South

Previous Station – Archway

Goal	Carriage	Door	Side
Exit	4	4	R

Hillingdon

Metropolitan **No of Carriages = 8**

Direction From –East

Previous Station – Ickenham

Goal	Carriage	Door	Side
Exit	7	1	L
Lift	8	2	L

Direction From – West

Previous Station – Uxbridge

Goal	Carriage	Door	Side
Exit	2	3	L
Lift	2	1	L

Piccadilly **No of Carriages = 6**

Direction From –East
Previous Station – Ickenham

Goal	Carriage	Door	Side
Exit	6	4	L

Direction From – West
Previous Station – Uxbridge

Goal	Carriage	Door	Side
Exit	2	4	L

Holborn

Central **No of Carriages = 8**

Direction From – East
Previous Station – Chancery Lane

Goal	Carriage	Door	Side
Exit	3	3	L
Piccadilly	3	3	L

Direction From – West
Previous Station – Tottenham Court Road

Goal	Carriage	Door	Side
Exit	6	1	L
Piccadilly	6	1	L

Piccadilly **No of Carriages = 6**

Direction From – North
Previous Station – Russell Square

Goal	Carriage	Door	Side
Central	1	2	L
Central	3	1	L
Exit	1	2	L
Exit	3	1	L

Direction From – South
Previous Station – Covent Garden

Goal	Carriage	Door	Side
Exit	4	2	L
Central	4	2	L

Holland Park

Central **No of Carriages = 8**

Direction From – East
Previous Station – Notting Hill Gate

Goal	Carriage	Door	Side
Exit	3	1	R

Direction From – West
Previous Station – Shepherd's Bush

Goal	Carriage	Door	Side
Exit	4	3	R

Holloway Road

Piccadilly **No of Carriages = 6**

Direction From – North
Previous Station – Arsenal

Goal	Carriage	Door	Side
Exit	5	1	R

Direction From – South
Previous Station – Caledonian Road

Goal	Carriage	Door	Side
Exit	2	3	R

Hornchurch

District **No of Carriages = 6**

Direction From – East
Previous Station – Upminster Bridge

Goal	Carriage	Door	Side
Exit	6	4	L

Direction From – West
Previous Station – Elm Park

Goal	Carriage	Door	Side
Exit	1	1	L

Hounslow Central

Piccadilly **No of Carriages = 6**

Direction From – East
Previous Station – Hounslow East

Goal	Carriage	Door	Side
Exit	1	1	R
Exit Lift	1	1	R

Direction From – West
Previous Station – Hounslow West

Goal	Carriage	Door	Side
Exit	6	4	R
Exit Lift	6	4	R

Hounslow East

Piccadilly **No of Carriages = 6**

Direction From – East
Previous Station – Osterley

Goal	Carriage	Door	Side
Exit	1	2	L

Direction From – West
Previous Station – Hounslow Central

Goal	Carriage	Door	Side
Exit	6	4	L

Hounslow West

Piccadilly **No of Carriages = 6**

Direction From – East
Previous Station – Hounslow Central

Goal	Carriage	Door	Side
Exit	1	4	R
Exit Lift	3	2	R

Direction From – West
Previous Station – Hatton Cross

Goal	Carriage	Door	Side
Exit	4	2	R
Exit Lift	6	2	R

Hyde Park Corner

Piccadilly **No of Carriages = 6**

Direction From – East
Previous Station – Green Park

Goal	Carriage	Door	Side
Exit	6	3/4	

Direction From – West
Previous Station – Knightsbridge

Goal	Carriage	Door	Side
Exit	1	1	

Ickenham

Metropolitan **No of Carriages = 8**

Direction From – East
Previous Station – Ruislip

Goal	Carriage	Door	Side
Exit	7	3	L

Direction From – West
Previous Station – Hillingdon

Goal	Carriage	Door	Side
Exit	1	3	L

Piccadilly **No of Carriages = 6**

Direction From – East
Previous Station – Ruislip

Goal	Carriage	Door	Side
Exit	6	4	L

Direction From – West
Previous Station – Hillingdon

Goal	Carriage	Door	Side
Exit	1	4	L

Kennington

Northern **No of Carriages = 6**

Direction From – North
Previous Station – Elephant & Castle/Waterloo

Goal	Carriage	Door	Side
Exit	5	3	L/R

Direction From – South
Previous Station – Oval

Goal	Carriage	Door	Side
Exit	3	2/3	L/R

Kensal Green

Bakerloo **No of Carriages = 7**

Direction From – North
Previous Station – Willesden Junction

Goal	Carriage	Door	Side
Exit	7	3	L

Direction From – South
Previous Station – Queen's Park

Goal	Carriage	Door	Side
Exit	1	1	L

Kensington (Olympia) *(Terminus)*

District **No of Carriages = 6**

Direction From – South
Previous Station – Earl's Court

Goal	Carriage	Door	Side
Exit	1	1	L
Rail	1	1	L

Kentish Town

Northern — **No of Carriages = 6**

Direction From – North
Previous Station – Tufnel Park

Goal	Carriage	Door	Side
Exit	2	3	L
Rail	2	3	L

Direction From – South
Previous Station – Camden Town

Goal	Carriage	Door	Side
Exit	4	2	R
Rail	4	2	R

Kenton

Bakerloo — **No of Carriages = 7**

Direction From – North
Previous Station – Harrow & Wealdstone

Goal	Carriage	Door	Side
Exit	7	3	L

Direction From – South
Previous Station – South Kenton

Goal	Carriage	Door	Side
Exit	1	1	L

Kew Gardens

District — **No of Carriages = 6**

Direction From – North
Previous Station – Gunnersbury

Goal	Carriage	Door	Side
Exit	3	4	L
Lift	4	1	L

Direction From – South
Previous Station – Richmond

Goal	Carriage	Door	Side
Exit	6	1	L
Lift (Via Subway)	6	1	L

Kilburn

Jubilee **No of Carriages = 7**

Direction From – North
Previous Station – Willesden Green

Goal	Carriage	Door	Side
Exit	1	1	R
Lift	1	1	R

Direction From – South
Previous Station – West Hampstead

Goal	Carriage	Door	Side
Lift	7	4	R
Exit	7	4	R

Kilburn Park

Bakerloo **No of Carriages = 7**

Direction From – North
Previous Station – Queen's Park

Goal	Carriage	Door	Side
Exit	3	1	R

Direction From – South
Previous Station – Maida Vale

Goal	Carriage	Door	Side
Exit	4	4	R

King's Cross St. Pancras

Circle **No of Carriages = 6**

Direction From – East
Previous Station – Farringdon

Goal	Carriage	Door	Side
Exit	1	1	R
Exit	4	4	R
Hammersmith & City	Any	Any	R
Lift	1	1	R
Metropolitan	Any	Any	R
Northern	6	4	R
Piccadilly	6	4	R
Rail	1	1	R
Rail	4	4	R
Victoria	6	4	R

Direction From – West
Previous Station – Euston Square

Goal	Carriage	Door	Side
Exit	3	1	R
Exit	6	3	R
Hammersmith & City	Any	Any	R
Lift	6	3	R
Metropolitan	Any	Any	R
Northern	1	1	R
Piccadilly	1	1	R
Rail	3	1	R
Rail	6	3	R
Victoria	1	1	R

Hammersmith & City **No of Carriages = 6**

Direction From – East
Previous Station – Farringdon

Goal	Carriage	Door	Side
Circle	Any	Any	R
Exit	2	2	R
Exit	4	3	R
Lift	2	2	R
Metropolitan	Any	Any	R
Northern	6	4	R
Piccadilly	6	4	R
Rail	2	2	R
Rail	4	3	R
Victoria	6	4	R

Direction From – West
Previous Station – Euston Square

Goal	Carriage	Door	Side
Circle	Any	Any	R
Exit	3	1	R
Exit	6	3	R
Lift	6	3	R
Metropolitan	Any	Any	R
Northern	1	1	R
Piccadilly	1	1	R
Rail	3	1	R
Rail	6	3	R
Victoria	1	1	R

King's Cross St. Pancras *(cont...)*

Metropolitan **No of Carriages = 8**

Direction From – East
Previous Station – Farringdon

Goal	Carriage	Door	Side
Circle	Any	Any	R
Exit	3	1	R
Exit	6	3	R
Hammersmith & City	Any	Any	R
Lift	3	1	R
Northern	8	3	R
Piccadilly	8	3	R
Rail	3	1	R
Rail	6	3	R
Victoria	8	3	R

Direction From – West
Previous Station – Euston Square

Goal	Carriage	Door	Side
Circle	Any	Any	R
Exit	3	1	R
Exit	6	2	R
Hammersmith & City	Any	Any	R
Lift	6	4	R
Northern	1	1	R
Piccadilly	1	1	R
Rail	3	1	R
Rail	6	2	R
Victoria	1	1	R

Northern **No of Carriages = 6**

Direction From – East
Previous Station – Angel

Goal	Carriage	Door	Side
Circle	5	4	R
Exit	5	4	R
Hammersmith & City	5	4	R
Metropolitan	5	4	R
Rail	5	4	R
Victoria	5	4	R

Direction From – West
Previous Station – Euston

Goal	Carriage	Door	Side
Circle	1	1	R
Exit	1	1	R
Hammersmith & City	1	1	R
Metropolitan	1	1	R
Rail	1	1	R
Victoria	1	1	R

Piccadilly **No of Carriages = 6**
Direction From – North
Previous Station – Caledonian Road

Goal	Carriage	Door	Side
Circle	1	1	R
Exit	1	1	R
Exit (Pentonville Rd)	6	3	R
Hammersmith & City	1	1	R
Metropolitan	1	1	R
Northern	1	1	R
Victoria	1	1	R

Direction From – South
Previous Station – Russell Square

Goal	Carriage	Door	Side
Circle	6	4	R
Exit	6	4	R
Exit (Pentonville Rd)	1	1	R
Hammersmith & City	6	4	R
Metropolitan	6	4	R
Northern	6	4	R
Victoria	6	4	R

King's Cross St. Pancras *(cont...)*

Victoria **No of Carriages = 8**

Direction From – North
Previous Station – Highbury & Islington

Goal	Carriage	Door	Side
Circle	1	1	L
Exit (Euston)	1	1	L
Exit (Pentonville Rd)	5	2	L
Lift	5	2	L
Hammersmith & City	1	1	L
Metropolitan	1	1	L
Northern	5	2	L
Northern	1	1	L
Piccadilly	5	2	L
Rail	5	2	L

Direction From – South
Previous Station – Euston

Goal	Carriage	Door	Side
Circle	8	3	L
Exit (Euston)	8	3	L
Lift	4	1/2	L
Exit (Pentonville Road)	2	1	L
Hammersmith & City	8	3	L
Metropolitan	8	3	L
Northern	8	3	L
Piccadilly	4	1/2	L
Rail	4	1/2	L

Kingsbury

Jubilee **No of Carriages = 7**

Direction From – North
Previous Station – Queensbury

Goal	Carriage	Door	Side
Exit	7	2	L

Direction From – South
Previous Station – Wembley Park

Goal	Carriage	Door	Side
Exit	1	3	L

Knightsbridge

Piccadilly — **No of Carriages = 6**

Direction From – East
Previous Station – Hyde Park Corner

Goal	Carriage	Door	Side
Exit (Brompton Rd & Harrods)	6	3	R
Exit (Sloane St & Knightsbridge)	3	1	R

Direction From – West
Previous Station – Gloucester Road

Goal	Carriage	Door	Side
Exit (Brompton Rd & Harrods)	1	1	R
Exit (Brompton Rd & Harrods)	4	1	R

Ladbroke Grove

Circle — **No of Carriages = 6**

Direction From – East
Previous Station – Westbourne Park

Goal	Carriage	Door	Side
Exit	6	1	L
Hammersmith & City	Any	Any	L

Direction From – West
Previous Station – Latimer Road

Goal	Carriage	Door	Side
Exit	1	4	L
Hammersmith & City	Any	Any	L

Hammersmith & City — **No of Carriages = 6**

Direction From – East
Previous Station – Westbourne Park

Goal	Carriage	Door	Side
Circle	Any	Any	L
Exit	6	1	L

Direction From – West
Previous Station – Latimer Road

Goal	Carriage	Door	Side
Circle	Any	Any	L
Exit	1	4	L

Lambeth North

Bakerloo **No of Carriages = 7**

Direction From – North
Previous Station – Waterloo

Goal	Carriage	Door	Side
Exit	7	3	R

Direction From – South
Previous Station – Elephant and Castle

Goal	Carriage	Door	Side
Exit	1	1	R

Lancaster Gate

Central **No of Carriages = 8**

Direction From – East
Previous Station – Marble Arch

Goal	Carriage	Door	Side
Exit	2	2	R

Direction From – West
Previous Station – Queensway

Goal	Carriage	Door	Side
Exit	6	1	R

Latimer Road

Circle **No of Carriages = 6**

Direction From – North
Previous Station – Ladbroke Road

Goal	Carriage	Door	Side
Exit	6	4	L
Hammersmith & City	Any	Any	L

Direction From – South
Previous Station – White City

Goal	Carriage	Door	Side
Exit	1	1	L
Hammersmith & City	Any	Any	L

Hammersmith & City **No of Carriages = 6**

Direction From – North

Previous Station – Ladbroke Road

Goal	Carriage	Door	Side
Circle	Any	Any	L
Exit	6	4	L

Direction From – South

Previous Station – White City

Goal	Carriage	Door	Side
Circle	Any	Any	L
Exit	1	1	L

Leicester Square

Northern **No of Carriages = 6**

Direction From – North

Previous Station – Tottenham Court Road

Goal	Carriage	Door	Side
Exit	3	4	R
Exit	3	1	R
Piccadilly	1	1	R
Piccadilly (Longer)	4	3	R

Direction From – South

Previous Station – Charing Cross

Goal	Carriage	Door	Side
Exit	3	1	R
Exit	3	4	R
Piccadilly	2	2	R
Piccadilly	6	6	R

Piccadilly **No of Carriages = 6**

Direction From – North

Previous Station – Covent Garden

Goal	Carriage	Door	Side
Exit	3	2/3	R
Northern	1	1	R

Direction From – South

Previous Station – Piccadilly Circus

Goal	Carriage	Door	Side
Exit	4	3	R
Northern	6	4	R

Leyton

Central **No of Carriages = 8**

Direction From – East
Previous Station – Leytonstone

Goal	Carriage	Door	Side
Exit	1	1	L

Direction From – West
Previous Station – Stratford

Goal	Carriage	Door	Side
Exit	8	3	L

Leytonstone

Central **No of Carriages = 8**

Direction From – East
Previous Station – Snaresbrook/Wanstead

Goal	Carriage	Door	Side
Snaresbrook	1	1	L/R
Wanstead	1	1	L/R
Exit	1	1	L/R

Direction From – West
Previous Station – Leyton

Goal	Carriage	Door	Side
Exit	8	3	L

Liverpool Street

Circle **No of Carriages = 6**

Direction From – East
Previous Station – Aldgate

Goal	Carriage	Door	Side
Central	3	3	L
Central	5	1	L
Central	6	2	L
Exit	3	3	L
Exit	5	1	L
Hammersmith & City	Any	Any	L
Metropolitan	Any	Any	L
Rail	3	3	L
Rail	5	1	L
Rail	6	2	L

Direction From – West
Previous Station – Moorgate

Goal	Carriage	Door	Side
Central	5	4	L
Exit	4	4	L
Hammersmith & City	Any	Any	L
Metropolitan	Any	Any	L
Rail	5	4	L

Central

No of Carriages = 8

Direction From – East
Previous Station – Bethnal Green

Goal	Carriage	Door	Side
Circle	8	1	R
Exit	8	1	R
Hammersmith & City	8	1	R
Metropolitan	8	1	R
Rail	8	1	R

Direction From – West
Previous Station – Bank

Goal	Carriage	Door	Side
Circle	2	1	R
Exit	2	1	R
Hammersmith & City	2	1	R
Metropolitan	2	1	R
Rail	2	1	R

Hammersmith & City

No of Carriages = 6

Direction From – East
Previous Station – Aldgate East

Goal	Carriage	Door	Side
Central	3	3	L
Central	5	1	L
Central	6	2	L
Circle	Any	Any	L
Exit	3	3	L
Exit	5	1	L
Metropolitan	Any	Any	L
Rail	3	3	L
Rail	5	1	L
Rail	6	2	L

Liverpool Street *(cont...)*

Hammersmith & City *(cont...)*

Direction From – West
Previous Station – Moorgate

Goal	Carriage	Door	Side
Central	5	4	L
Circle	Any	Any	L
Exit	4	4	L
Metropolitan	Any	Any	L
Rail	5	4	L

Metropolitan

No of Carriages = 8

Direction From – East
Previous Station – Aldgate

Goal	Carriage	Door	Side
Central	4	3	L
Central	6	2	L
Circle	Any	Any	L
Exit	3	2	L
Exit	4	3	L
Hammersmith & City	Any	Any	L
Rail	4	3	L
Rail	6	2	L

Direction From – West
Previous Station – Moorgate

Goal	Carriage	Door	Side
Central	5	3	L
Circle	Any	Any	L
Exit	5	3	L
Exit	4	4	L
Hammersmith & City	Any	Any	L
Rail	5	3	L
Rail	4	4	L

London Bridge

Jubilee

No of Carriages = 7

Direction From – East
Previous Station – Bermondsey

Goal	Carriage	Door	Side
Exit	4	3	R
Exit (Borough High St.)	2	1	R
Lift	7	3	R
Northern	3	4	R
Rail	4	3	R

Direction From – West
Previous Station – Southwark

Goal	Carriage	Door	Side
Exit	4	3	R
Exit (Borough High St.)	7	1	R
Lift	1	1	R
Northern	5	1	R
Rail	4	3	R

Northern

No of Carriages = 6

Direction From – North
Previous Station – Bank

Goal	Carriage	Door	Side
Exit	3	3	L
Exit	5	2/3	L
Exit (Borough High St.)	2	2	L
Jubilee	2	2	L
Lift	1	2	L
Rail	3	3	L
Rail	5	2/3	L

Direction From – South
Previous Station – Borough

Goal	Carriage	Door	Side
Exit	3	1	L
Exit	4	2	L
Exit (Borough High St.)	6	1	L
Jubilee	6	1	L
Lift	6	4	L
Rail	3	1	L
Rail	4	2	L

Loughton

Central **No of Carriages = 8**

Direction From – North
Previous Station – Debden

Goal	Carriage	Door	Side
Exit	3	3	R
Exit & terminates	3	3	L

Direction From – South
Previous Station – Buckhurst Hill

Goal	Carriage	Door	Side
Exit & terminates	6	4	L
Exit	6	4	R

Maida Vale

Bakerloo **No of Carriages = 7**

Direction From – North
Previous Station – Kilburn Park

Goal	Carriage	Door	Side
Exit	4	3	R

Direction From – South
Previous Station – Warwick Avenue

Goal	Carriage	Door	Side
Exit	3	4	R

Manor House

Piccadilly **No of Carriages = 6**

Direction From – North
Previous Station – Turnpike Lane

Goal	Carriage	Door	Side
Exit	4	3	R

Direction From – South
Previous Station – Finsbury Park

Goal	Carriage	Door	Side
Exit	2	4	R

Mansion House

Circle **No of Carriages = 6**

Direction From – East
Previous Station – Cannon Street

Goal	Carriage	Door	Side
Exit	6	3	R

Direction From – West
Previous Station – Blackfriars

Goal	Carriage	Door	Side
Exit	4	1	L

District **No of Carriages = 6**

Direction From – East
Previous Station – Cannon Street

Goal	Carriage	Door	Side
Exit	5	4	R

Direction From – West
Previous Station – Blackfriars

Goal	Carriage	Door	Side
Exit	3	3	L

Marble Arch

Central **No of Carriages = 8**

Direction From – East
Previous Station – Bond Street

Goal	Carriage	Door	Side
Exit	5	2	R

Direction From – West
Previous Station – Lancaster Gate

Goal	Carriage	Door	Side
Exit	4	2	R

Marylebone

Bakerloo **No of Carriages = 7**

Direction From – East
Previous Station – Baker Street

Goal	Carriage	Door	Side
Exit	4	3	L
Rail	4	3	L

Direction From – West
Previous Station – Edgware Road

Goal	Carriage	Door	Side
Exit	5	3	L
Rail	5	3	L

Mile End

Central **No of Carriages = 8**

Direction From – East
Previous Station – Stratford

Goal	Carriage	Door	Side
District (East-Bound)	4	3	R
District (West-Bound)	Any	Any	R
Exit	4	3	R
Hammersmith & City (E'-Bound)	4	3	R
Hammersmith & City (W'-Bound)	Any	Any	R

Direction From – West
Previous Station – Bethnal Green

Goal	Carriage	Door	Side
District (East-Bound)	Any	Any	R
District (West-Bound)	5	3	R
Exit	5	3	R
Hammersmith & City (E'-Bound)	Any	Any	R
Hammersmith & City (W'-Bound)	5	3	R

District **No of Carriages = 6**

Direction From – East
Previous Station – Bow Road

Goal	Carriage	Door	Side
Central (East-Bound)	4	2	R
Central (West-Bound)	Any	Any	R
Exit	4	2	R

Direction From – West
Previous Station – Stepney Green

Goal	Carriage	Door	Side
Central (East-Bound)	Any	Any	L
Central (West-Bound)	5	2	L
Exit	5	2	L

Hammersmith & City **No of Carriages = 6**

Direction From – East
Previous Station – Bow Road

Goal	Carriage	Door	Side
Central (East-Bound)	4	2	L
Central (West-Bound)	Any	Any	L
Exit	4	2	L

Direction From – West
Previous Station – Stepney Green

Goal	Carriage	Door	Side
Central (East-Bound)	Any	Any	L
Central (West-Bound)	5	3	L
Exit	5	3	L

Mill Hill East *(Terminus)*

Northern **No of Carriages = 6**

Direction From – South
Previous Station – Finchley Central

Goal	Carriage	Door	Side
Exit	4	3	R

Monument

District & Circle **No of Carriages = 6**

Direction From – East
Previous Station – Tower Hill

Goal	Carriage	Door	Side
DLR	3	1	L
Exit	3	1	L
Northern	1	1	L
Waterloo & City	3	1	L

Monument *(cont...)*

District & **Circle** *(cont...)* **No of Carriages = 6**

Direction From – West

Previous Station – Monument

Goal	Carriage	Door	Side
DLR	4	2	L
DLR	6	2	L
Exit	2	2	L
Exit	6	2	L
Northern	6	4	L
Waterloo & City	4	2	L
Waterloo & City	6	2	L

Moor Park

Metropolitan **No of Carriages = 8**

Direction From – North

Previous Station – Croxley/Rickmansworth

Goal	Carriage	Door	Side
Exit	4	2	R
Exit	4	2	R
North (other branch)	4	2	R

Direction From – South

Previous Station – Northwood

Goal	Carriage	Door	Side
Exit	5	2	R
Exit	5	2	R

Moorgate

Circle **No of Carriages = 6**

Direction From – East

Previous Station – Liverpool Street

Goal	Carriage	Door	Side
Central	6	4	L
Exit	6	4	L
Hammersmith & City	Any	Any	L
Metropolitan	Any	Any	L
Northern	6	4	L
Rail	6	4	L

Direction From – West
Previous Station – Barbican

Goal	Carriage	Door	Side
Central	1	4	L
Exit	1	4	L
Hammersmith & City	Any	Any	L
Metropolitan	Any	Any	L
Northern	1	4	L
Rail	1	4	L

Hammersmith & City

No of Carriages = 6

Direction From – East
Previous Station – Liverpool Street

Goal	Carriage	Door	Side
Central	6	4	L
Exit	6	4	L
Hammersmith & City	Any	Any	L
Metropolitan	Any	Any	L
Northern	6	4	L
Rail	6	4	L

Direction From – West
Previous Station – Barbican

Goal	Carriage	Door	Side
Central	1	4	L
Exit	1	4	L
Hammersmith & City	Any	Any	L
Metropolitan	Any	Any	L
Northern	1	4	L
Rail	1	4	L

Metropolitan

No of Carriages = 8

Direction From – East
Previous Station – Liverpool Street

Goal	Carriage	Door	Side
Central	8	2	L
Exit	8	2	L
Hammersmith & City	Any	Any	L
Metropolitan	Any	Any	L
Northern	8	2	L
Rail	8	2	L

Moorgate *(cont...)*

Metropolitan *(cont...)* **No of Carriages = 8**

Direction From – West
Previous Station – Barbican

Goal	Carriage	Door	Side
Central	1	4	L
Exit	1	4	L
Hammersmith & City	Any	Any	L
Metropolitan	Any	Any	L
Northern	1	4	L
Rail	1	4	L

Northern **No of Carriages = 6**

Direction From – North
Previous Station – Old Street

Goal	Carriage	Door	Side
Circle	3	3	R
Exit	3	3	R
Hammersmith & City	3	3	R
Metropolitan	3	3	R
Rail (Bedford)	3	3	R
Rail (Stevenage)	5	4	R

Direction From – South
Previous Station – Bank

Goal	Carriage	Door	Side
Circle	4	3	R
Exit	4	3	R
Hammersmith & City	4	3	R
Metropolitan	4	3	R
Rail (Bedford)	4	3	R
Rail (Stevenage)	5	4	R

Morden *(Terminus)*

Northern **No of Carriages = 6**

Direction From – North
Previous Station – South Wimbledon

Goal	Carriage	Door	Side
Exit	3	2/3	L/R
Lift	4	2	L/R

Mornington Crescent

Northern — **No of Carriages = 6**

Direction From – North
Previous Station – Camden Town

Goal	Carriage	Door	Side
Exit	3	1	R

Direction From – South
Previous Station – Euston

Goal	Carriage	Door	Side
Exit	4	2	R

Neasden

Jubilee — **No of Carriages = 7**

Direction From – North
Previous Station – Wembley Park

Goal	Carriage	Door	Side
Exit	1	1	R

Direction From – South
Previous Station – Dollis Hill

Goal	Carriage	Door	Side
Exit	7	3	R

Newbury Park

Central — **No of Carriages = 8**

Direction From – North
Previous Station – Barkingside

Goal	Carriage	Door	Side
Exit	4	4	L

Direction From – South
Previous Station – Gants Hill

Goal	Carriage	Door	Side
Exit	4	1	L

North Acton

Central — **No of Carriages = 8**

Direction From – East
Previous Station – East Acton

Goal	Carriage	Door	Side
Exit	5	2	L

Direction From – West
Previous Station – West Acton/Hangar Lane
Platform 2 (Left) Platform 3 (Right)

Goal	Carriage	Door	Side
Central Line Westwards	5	2	L/R
Exit	5	2	L/R

North Ealing

Piccadilly — **No of Carriages = 6**

Direction From – North
Previous Station – Park Royal

Goal	Carriage	Door	Side
Exit (via Bridge)	3	1	L

Direction From – South
Previous Station – Ealing Common

Goal	Carriage	Door	Side
Exit	6	4	L

North Greenwich

Jubilee — **No of Carriages = 7**

Direction From – East
Previous Station – Canning Town

Goal	Carriage	Door	Side
Exit	1	1	L
Exit	7	2	L
Lift	4	1	L

Direction From – West
Previous Station – Canary Wharf

Goal	Carriage	Door	Side
Exit	1	3	L/R
Exit	7	3	L/R
Lift	4	1	L/R

North Harrow

Metropolitan **No of Carriages = 8**

Direction From – North
Previous Station – Pinner

Goal	Carriage	Door	Side
Exit	1	3	L

Direction From – South
Previous Station – Harrow-on-the-Hill

Goal	Carriage	Door	Side
Exit	8	1	L

North Wembley

Bakerloo **No of Carriages = 7**

Direction From – North
Previous Station – South Kenton

Goal	Carriage	Door	Side
Exit	7	3	L

Direction From – South
Previous Station – Wembley Central

Goal	Carriage	Door	Side
Exit	1	1	L

Northfields

Piccadilly **No of Carriages = 6**

Direction From – East
Previous Station – South Ealing

Goal	Carriage	Door	Side
Exit	1	1	L/R

Direction From – West
Previous Station – Boston Manor

Goal	Carriage	Door	Side
Exit	6	4	L/R

Northolt

Central **No of Carriages = 8**

Direction From – North
Previous Station – South Ruislip

Goal	Carriage	Door	Side
Exit	1	2	R

Direction From – South
Previous Station – Greenford

Goal	Carriage	Door	Side
Exit	8	1	R8

Northwick Park

Metropolitan **No of Carriages = 8**

Direction From – East
Previous Station – Preston Road

Goal	Carriage	Door	Side
Exit	2	3	R

Direction From – West
Previous Station – Harrow-on-the-Hill

Goal	Carriage	Door	Side
Exit	6	3	R

Northwood

Metropolitan **No of Carriages = 8**

Direction From – North
Previous Station – Moor Park

Goal	Carriage	Door	Side
Exit	7	1	L

Direction From – South
Previous Station – Northwood Hills

Goal	Carriage	Door	Side
Exit	3	2	L

Northwood Hills

Metropolitan **No of Carriages = 8**

Direction From – North
Previous Station – Northwood

Goal	Carriage	Door	Side
Exit	8	2	L

Direction From – South
Previous Station – Pinner

Goal	Carriage	Door	Side
Exit	1	2	L

Notting Hill Gate

Central **No of Carriages = 8**

Direction From – East
Previous Station – Queensway

Goal	Carriage	Door	Side
District & Circle	8	3	R
Exit	8	3	R

Direction From – West
Previous Station – Holland Park

Goal	Carriage	Door	Side
District & Circle	1	1	L
Exit	1	1	L

District & Circle **No of Carriages = 6**

Direction From – North
Previous Station – Bayswater

Goal	Carriage	Door	Side
Central	5	3	L
Exit	6	3	L

Direction From – South
Previous Station – High Street Kensington

Goal	Carriage	Door	Side
Central	1	3	L
Exit	2	3	L

Oakwood

Piccadilly **No of Carriages = 6**

Direction From – North
Previous Station – Cockfosters

Goal	Carriage	Door	Side
Exit	6	2	R
Exit Lift	5	3	R

Direction From – South
Previous Station – Southgate

Goal	Carriage	Door	Side
Exit	2	1	R
Exit Lift	2	3	R

Old Street

Northern **No of Carriages = 6**

Direction From – North
Previous Station – Angel

Goal	Carriage	Door	Side
Exit	2	3	R
Exit	5	4	R
Rail	6	3	R

Direction From – South
Previous Station – Moorgate

Goal	Carriage	Door	Side
Exit	1	3	R
Exit	3	2/3	R
Rail	1	1	R

Osterley

Piccadilly **No of Carriages = 6**

Direction From – East
Previous Station – Boston Manor

Goal	Carriage	Door	Side
Exit	2	2	L

Direction From – West
Previous Station – Hounslow East

Goal	Carriage	Door	Side
Exit	6	2	L

Oval

Northern **No of Carriages = 6**

Direction From – North
Previous Station – Kennington

Goal	Carriage	Door	Side
Exit	1	1	R

Direction From – South
Previous Station – Stockwell

Goal	Carriage	Door	Side
Exit	3	1	L

Oxford Circus

Bakerloo **No of Carriages = 7**

Direction From – North
Previous Station – Regent's Park

Goal	Carriage	Door	Side
Central	2	4	L
Exit	1	4	L
Victoria (North-Bound)	6	4	L
Victoria (South-Bound)	4	2	L

Direction From – South
Previous Station – Piccadilly Circus

Goal	Carriage	Door	Side
Central	5	3	L
Exit	6	4	L
Victoria (North-Bound)	4	4	L
Victoria (South-Bound)	1	2	L

Oxford Circus *(cont...)*

Central **No of Carriages = 8**

Direction From – East
Previous Station – Tottenham Court Road

Goal	Carriage	Door	Side
Bakerloo	1	1	R
Exit	1	1	R
Exit (Street Only)	4	2	R
Exit (Street Only)	5	3	R
Victoria	1	1	R

Direction From – West
Previous Station – Bond Street

Goal	Carriage	Door	Side
Bakerloo	8	3	R
Exit (Street Only)	3	4	R
Exit (Street Only)	5	1	R
Exit	8	3	R
Victoria	8	3	R

Victoria **No of Carriages = 8**

Direction From – North
Previous Station – Warren Street

Goal	Carriage	Door	Side
Bakerloo (North-Bound)	6	2	R
Bakerloo (South-Bound)	4	2/3	R
Central	2	2	R
Exit	2	2	R

Direction From – South
Previous Station – Green Park

Goal	Carriage	Door	Side
Bakerloo (North-Bound)	5	1	R
Bakerloo (North-Bound)	8	2	R
Bakerloo (South-Bound)	2	3	R
Central	6	3	R
Exit	7	2	R

Paddington

Bakerloo **No of Carriages = 7**

Direction From – North
Previous Station – Warwick Avenue

Goal	Carriage	Door	Side
Circle (H'smith or Victoria)	3	2	R
District	3	2	R
Exit	3	2	R
Hammersmith & City	3	2	R
Rail	3	2	R

Direction From – South
Previous Station – Edgware Road

Goal	Carriage	Door	Side
Circle (H'smith or Victoria)	4	2	R
District	4	2	R
Exit	4	2	R
Hammersmith & City	4	2	R
Rail	4	2	R

Circle ***Hammersmith Branch*** **No of Carriages = 6**

Direction From – East
Previous Station – Edgware Road
Paddington *Platform 15*

Goal	Carriage	Door	Side
Bakerloo	5	2	R
Circle (Victoria Branch)	5	2	R
District	5	2	R
Exit	5	2	R
Hammersmith & City	Any	Any	R
Rail	5	2	R

Direction From – West
Previous Station – Royal Oak
Paddington Platform 15

Goal	Carriage	Door	Side
Bakerloo	2	4	R
Circle (Victoria Branch)	2	4	R
District	2	4	R
Exit	2	4	R
Hammersmith & City	Any	Any	R
Rail	2		R

Paddington *(cont...)*

Circle ***Victoria Branch*** **No of Carriages = 6**

Direction From – East
Previous Station – Edgware Road

Goal	Carriage	Door	Side
Bakerloo	3	1	L
District	Any	Any	L
Exit	3	1	L
Exit (Praed St)	5	1	L
Hammersmith & City	3	1	L
Rail	3	1	L

Direction From – South
Previous Station – Bayswater

Goal	Carriage	Door	Side
Bakerloo	4	3	L
District	Any	Any	L
Exit	4	3	L
Exit (Praed Street)	2	2	L
Hammersmith & City	4	3	L
Rail	4	3	L

District **No of Carriages = 6**

Direction From – East
Previous Station – Edgware Road

Goal	Carriage	Door	Side
Bakerloo	3	1	L
Circle	Any	Any	L
Exit	3	1	L
Exit (Praed St)	5	2	L
Hammersmith & City	3	1	L
Rail	3	1	L

Direction From – West
Previous Station – Bayswater

Goal	Carriage	Door	Side
Bakerloo	4	3	L
Circle	Any	Any	L
Exit	4	3	L
Exit (Praed St)	2	2	L
Hammersmith & City	4	3	L
Rail	4	3	L

Hammersmith & City No of Carriages = 6

Direction From – East
Previous Station – Edgware Road

Goal	Carriage	Door	Side
Bakerloo	5	2	R
Circle	Any	Any	R
Circle (Victoria Branch)	5	2	R
District	5	2	R
Exit	5	2	R
Rail	5	2	R

Direction From –West
Previous Station – Royal Oak

Goal	Carriage	Door	Side
Bakerloo	2	4	R
Circle	Any	Any	R
Circle (Victoria Branch)	2	4	R
District	2	4	R
Exit	2	4	R
Rail	2	4	R

Park Royal

Piccadilly No of Carriages = 6

Direction From – North
Previous Station – Alperton

Goal	Carriage	Door	Side
Exit	6	4	L

Direction From – South
Previous Station – North Ealing

Goal	Carriage	Door	Side
Exit	1	1	L

Parsons Green

District **No of Carriages = 6**

Direction From – North
Previous Station – Fulham Broadway

Goal	Carriage	Door	Side
Exit	5	4	L

Direction From – South
Previous Station – Putney Bridge

Goal	Carriage	Door	Side
Exit	1	2	L

Perivale

Central **No of Carriages = 8**

Direction From – East
Previous Station – Hangar Lane

Goal	Carriage	Door	Side
Exit	8	3	R

Direction From – West
Previous Station – Greenford

Goal	Carriage	Door	Side
Exit	1	1	R

Piccadilly Circus

Bakerloo **No of Carriages = 7**

Direction From – North
Previous Station – Oxford Circus

Goal	Carriage	Door	Side
Exit	5	2	L
Piccadilly	3	3	L

Direction From – South
Previous Station – Charing Cross

Goal	Carriage	Door	Side
Exit	4	3	L
Piccadilly	5	3	L

Piccadilly **No of Carriages = 6**

Direction From – North
Previous Station – Leicester Square

Goal	Carriage	Door	Side
Bakerloo	3	2	R
Exit	2	2	R

Direction From – South
Previous Station – Green Park

Goal	Carriage	Door	Side
Bakerloo	1	1	R
Exit	2	1/2	R

Pimlico

Victoria **No of Carriages = 8**

Direction From – North
Previous Station – Victoria

Goal	Carriage	Door	Side
Exit	3	1	R

Direction From – South
Previous Station – Vauxhall

Goal	Carriage	Door	Side
Exit	6	3/4	R

Pinner

Metropolitan **No of Carriages = 8**

Direction From – North
Previous Station – Northwood Hills

Goal	Carriage	Door	Side
Exit	4	3	L
Lift	1	3	L

Direction From – South
Previous Station – North Harrow

Goal	Carriage	Door	Side
Exit	6	1	L
Lift	8	1	L

Plaistow

District **No of Carriages = 6**

Direction From – East
Previous Station – Upton Park

Goal	Carriage	Door	Side
Exit	6	4	L

Direction From – West
Previous Station – West Ham

Goal	Carriage	Door	Side
Exit	2	1	L

Hammersmith & City **No of Carriages = 6**

Direction From – East
Previous Station – Upton Park

Goal	Carriage	Door	Side
Exit	6	4	L
Exit	2	1	L

Direction From – West
Previous Station – West Ham

Goal	Carriage	Door	Side
Exit	1	1	R
District (East-Bound)	1/2	Any	R

Preston Road

Metropolitan **No of Carriages = 8**

Direction From – East
Previous Station – Wembley Park

Goal	Carriage	Door	Side
Exit	8	4	R

Direction From – West
Previous Station – Northwick Park

Goal	Carriage	Door	Side
Exit	1	1	R

Putney Bridge

District **No of Carriages = 6**

Direction From – North
Previous Station – Parsons Green

Goal	Carriage	Door	Side
Exit	3	1	L
Exit	2	2	L

Direction From – South
Previous Station – East Putney

Goal	Carriage	Door	Side
Exit	6	1	L

Queen's Park

Bakerloo **No of Carriages = 7**

Direction From – North
Previous Station – Kensal Green

Goal	Carriage	Door	Side
Exit	1	1	L
Rail	Any	Any	L

Direction From – South
Previous Station – Kilburn Park

Goal	Carriage	Door	Side
Exit	7	3	L
Rail	Any	Any	L

Queensbury

Jubilee **No of Carriages = 7**

Direction From – North
Previous Station – Canons Park

Goal	Carriage	Door	Side
Exit	3	1	L

Direction From – South
Previous Station – Kingsbury

Goal	Carriage	Door	Side
Exit	5	4	L

Queensway

Central **No of Carriages = 8**

Direction From – East
Previous Station – Lancaster Gate

Goal	Carriage	Door	Side
Exit	6	3	R

Direction From – West
Previous Station – Notting Hill Gate

Goal	Carriage	Door	Side
Exit	3	1	R

Ravenscourt Park

District — **No of Carriages = 6**

Direction From – East
Previous Station – Hammersmith

Goal	Carriage	Door	Side
Exit	2	4	R

Direction From – West
Previous Station – Stamford Brook

Goal	Carriage	Door	Side
Exit	4	3	R

Rayners Lane

Metropolitan — **No of Carriages = 8**

Direction From – East
Previous Station – West Harrow

Goal	Carriage	Door	Side
Exit	7	1	L
Piccadilly Southwards	7	1	L

Direction From – West
Previous Station – Eastcote

Goal	Carriage	Door	Side
Exit	2	2	L

Piccadilly — **No of Carriages = 6**

Direction From – North
Previous Station – Eastcote

Goal	Carriage	Door	Side
Exit	2	2	L

Direction From – South
Previous Station – South Harrow

Goal	Carriage	Door	Side
Exit	6	4	L
Metropolitan Eastwards	6	4	L

Redbridge

Central

No of Carriages = 8

Direction From –East
Previous Station – Gants Hill

Goal	Carriage	Door	Side
Exit	1	1	R

Direction From – West
Previous Station – Wanstead

Goal	Carriage	Door	Side
Exit	8	3	R

Regent's Park

Bakerloo

No of Carriages = 7

Direction From – North
Previous Station – Baker Street

Goal	Carriage	Door	Side
Exit	4	3	R

Direction From – South
Previous Station – Oxford Circus

Goal	Carriage	Door	Side
Exit	3	4	L

Richmond *(Terminus)*

District

No of Carriages = 6

Direction From – North
Previous Station – Kew Gardens

Goal	Carriage	Door	Side
Exit	1	1	L/R
Lift	1	1	L/R
Rail	1	1	L/R

Rickmansworth

Metropolitan

No of Carriages = 8

Direction From – East
Previous Station – Moor Park

Goal	Carriage	Door	Side
Exit	5	3	L

Direction From – West
Previous Station – Chorley Wood

Goal	Carriage	Door	Side
Exit	5	1	L

Roding Valley

Central

No of Carriages = 8

Direction From – East
Previous Station – Chigwell

Goal	Carriage	Door	Side
Exit	4	2	L

Direction From – South
Previous Station – Woodford

Goal	Carriage	Door	Side
Exit	6	2	L

Royal Oak

Circle

No of Carriages = 6

Direction From – North
Previous Station – Paddington

Goal	Carriage	Door	Side
Exit	1	1	L
Hammersmith & City	Any	Any	L

Direction From – South
Previous Station – Westbourne Park

Goal	Carriage	Door	Side
Exit	6	4	L
Hammersmith & City	Any	Any	L

Hammersmith & City **No of Carriages = 6**

Direction From – North
Previous Station – Paddington

Goal	Carriage	Door	Side
Circle	Any	Any	L
Exit	1	1	L

Direction From – South
Previous Station – Westbourne Park

Goal	Carriage	Door	Side
Circle	Any	Any	L
Exit	6	4	L

Ruislip

Metropolitan **No of Carriages = 8**

Direction From – East
Previous Station – Ruislip Manor

Goal	Carriage	Door	Side
Exit (via Bridge)	4	3	L

Direction From – West
Previous Station – Ickenham

Goal	Carriage	Door	Side
Exit	4	3	L

Piccadilly **No of Carriages = 6**

Direction From – East
Previous Station – Ruislip Manor

Goal	Carriage	Door	Side
Exit	4	4	L

Direction From – West
Previous Station – Ickenham

Goal	Carriage	Door	Side
Exit	4	2	L

Ruislip Gardens

Central **No of Carriages = 8**

Direction From – North
Previous Station – West Ruislip

Goal	Carriage	Door	Side
Exit	5	3	R

Direction From – South
Previous Station – South Ruislip

Goal	Carriage	Door	Side
Exit	4	2	R

Ruislip Manor

Metropolitan **No of Carriages = 8**

Direction From – East
Previous Station – Eastcote

Goal	Carriage	Door	Side
Exit	1	2	L

Direction From – West
Previous Station – Ruislip

Goal	Carriage	Door	Side
Exit	8	2	L

Piccadilly **No of Carriages = 6**

Direction From – East
Previous Station – Eastcote

Goal	Carriage	Door	Side
Exit	1	3	L

Direction From – West
Previous Station – Ruislip

Goal	Carriage	Door	Side
Exit	6	1	L

Russell Square

Piccadilly **No of Carriages = 6**

Direction From – North
Previous Station – King's Cross St. Pancras

Goal	Carriage	Door	Side
Exit	1	1	L

Direction From – South
Previous Station –Holborn

Goal	Carriage	Door	Side
Exit	6	4	L

Seven Sisters

Victoria **No of Carriages = 8**
Direction From – North
Previous Station – Tottenham Hale

Goal	Carriage	Door	Side
Exit (Seven Sisters Road)	2	2	R
Exit (Buses/High Road)	7	2/3	R
Rail	2	2	R

Direction From – South
Previous Station – Finsbury Park

Goal	Carriage	Door	Side
Exit (Buses/High Road)	2	2	L/R
Exit (Seven Sisters Road)	7	3	L/R
Rail	7	3	L/R
Victoria (Continue Northwards)	7	3	L/Rs

Shepherd's Bush

Central **No of Carriages = 8**
Direction From – East
Previous Station – Holland Park

Goal	Carriage	Door	Side
Exit	1	1	R

Direction From – West
Previous Station – White City

Goal	Carriage	Door	Side
Exit	7	3	R

Shepherd's Bush Market

Circle **No of Carriages = 6**

Direction From – North
Previous Station – Woods Lane

Goal	Carriage	Door	Side
Exit	1	1	L
Hammersmith & City	Any	Any	L

Direction From – South
Previous Station – Goldhawk Road

Goal	Carriage	Door	Side
Exit	6	4	L
Hammersmith & City	Any	Any	L

Hammersmith & City **No of Carriages = 6**

Direction From – North
Previous Station – Woods Lane

Goal	Carriage	Door	Side
Exit	1	1h	L
Circle	Any	Any	L

Direction From – South
Previous Station – Goldhawk Road

Goal	Carriage	Door	Side
Exit	6	4	L
Circle	Any	Any	L

Sloane Square

Circle **No of Carriages = 6**

Direction From – East
Previous Station – Victoria

Goal	Carriage	Door	Side
Exit	2	4	L
Exit	3	1	L

Direction From – West
Previous Station – South Kensington

Goal	Carriage	Door	Side
Exit	5	1	L
Exit	5	3	L

District **No of Carriages = 6**

Direction From – East
Previous Station – Victoria

Goal	Carriage	Door	Side
Exit	2	3	L
Exit	3	1	L

Direction From – West
Previous Station – South Kensington

Goal	Carriage	Door	Side
Exit	4	3	L
Exit	5	1	L

Snaresbrook

Central **No of Carriages = 8**

Direction From – North
Previous Station – South Woodford

Goal	Carriage	Door	Side
Exit	7	2	L

Direction From – South
Previous Station – Leytonstone

Goal	Carriage	Door	Side
Exit	1	1	L

South Ealing

Piccadilly **No of Carriages = 6**

Direction From – East
Previous Station – Acton Town

Goal	Carriage	Door	Side
Exit	6	4	L/R

Direction From – West
Previous Station – Northfields

Goal	Carriage	Door	Side
Exit	1	1	L/R

South Harrow

Piccadilly **No of Carriages = 6**

Direction From – North
Previous Station – Rayners Lane

Goal	Carriage	Door	Side
Exit	6	4	L

Direction From – South
Previous Station – Sudbury Hill

Goal	Carriage	Door	Side
Exit	1	1	L

South Kensington

District & Circle **No of Carriages = 6**

Direction From – East
Previous Station – Sloane Square

Goal	Carriage	Door	Side
Exit	3	2	R
Piccadilly	3	1	R
Piccadilly	5	1	R

Direction From – West
Previous Station – Gloucester Road

Goal	Carriage	Door	Side
Exit	6	4	R
Piccadilly	3	4	R
Piccadilly	5	3	R

Piccadilly **No of Carriages = 6**

Direction From – East
Previous Station – Knightsbridge

Goal	Carriage	Door	Side
District & Circle	2	4	L
Exit	2	4	L

Direction From – West
Previous Station – Gloucester Road

Goal	Carriage	Door	Side
District & Circle	3	3/4	R
Exit	3	3/4	R

South Kenton

Bakerloo **No of Carriages = 7**

Direction From – North
Previous Station – Kenton

Goal	Carriage	Door	Side
Exit	7	3	R

Direction From – South
Previous Station – North Wembley

Goal	Carriage	Door	Side
Exit	1	1	R

South Ruislip

Central **No of Carriages = 8**

Direction From – North
Previous Station – Ruislip Gardens

Goal	Carriage	Door	Side
Exit	2	4	R
Rail	2	4	R

Direction From – South
Previous Station – Northolt

Goal	Carriage	Door	Side
Exit	6	3	R
Rail	6	3	R

South Wimbledon

Northern **No of Carriages = 6**

Direction From – North
Previous Station – Colliers Wood

Goal	Carriage	Door	Side
Exit	4	2	R

Direction From – South
Previous Station – Morden

Goal	Carriage	Door	Side
Exit	3	3	R

South Woodford

Central **No of Carriages = 8**

Direction From – North
Previous Station – Woodford

Goal	Carriage	Door	Side
Exit	8	3	L

Direction From – South
Previous Station – Snaresbrook

Goal	Carriage	Door	Side
Exit	1	1	L

Southfields

District **No of Carriages = 6**

Direction From – North
Previous Station – East Putney

Goal	Carriage	Door	Side
Exit	1	1	R
Lift	1	1	R

Direction From – South
Previous Station – Wimbledon Park

Goal	Carriage	Door	Side
Exit	6	4	R
Lift	6	4	R

Southgate

Piccadilly **No of Carriages = 6**

Direction From – North
Previous Station – Oakwood

Goal	Carriage	Door	Side
Exit	3	3	R

Direction From – South
Previous Station – Arnos Grove

Goal	Carriage	Door	Side
Exit	4	2	R

Southwark

Jubilee **No of Carriages = 7**

Direction From – East
Previous Station – London Bridge

Goal	Carriage	Door	Side
Exit	2	3	R
Exit	5	3	R
Lift	2	2	R
Rail	2	3	R
Rail	5	3	R

Direction From – West
Previous Station – Waterloo

Goal	Carriage	Door	Side
Exit	3	3	R
Exit	5	2/3	R
Lift	7	3	R
Rail	3	3	R
Rail	5	2/3	R

St. James's Park

District & **Circle** **No of Carriages = 6**

Direction From – East
Previous Station – Westminster

Goal	Carriage	Door	Side
Exit (Park & Broadway)	6	4	L
Exit (Victoria St.)	2	4	L

Direction From – West
Previous Station – Victoria

Goal	Carriage	Door	Side
Exit (Park & Broadway)	2	2	L
Exit (Victoria St.)	6	4	L

St. Paul's

Central **No of Carriages = 8**

Direction From – East
Previous Station – Bank

Goal	Carriage	Door	Side
Exit	8	3	R

Direction From – West
Previous Station – Chancery Lane

Goal	Carriage	Door	Side
Exit	3	1	L

St. John's Wood

Jubilee **No of Carriages = 7**

Direction From – North
Previous Station – Swiss Cottage

Goal	Carriage	Door	Side
Exit	3	4	R

Direction From – South
Previous Station – Baker Street

Goal	Carriage	Door	Side
Exit	5	2	R

Stamford Brook

District **No of Carriages = 6**

Direction From – East
Previous Station – Ravenscourt Park

Goal	Carriage	Door	Side
Exit	5	3	R

Direction From – West
Previous Station – Turnham Green

Goal	Carriage	Door	Side
Exit	1	1	L

Stanmore *(Terminus)*

Jubilee **No of Carriages = 7**

Direction From – South
Previous Station – Canons Park

Goal	Carriage	Door	Side
Exit	1	1	R

Stepney Green

District — **No of Carriages = 6**

Direction From – East
Previous Station – Mile End

Goal	Carriage	Door	Side
Exit	5	4	L

Direction From – West
Previous Station – Whitechapel

Goal	Carriage	Door	Side
Exit	2	3	L

Hammersmith & City — **No of Carriages = 6**

Direction From – East
Previous Station – Mile End

Goal	Carriage	Door	Side
Exit	6	4	L

Direction From – West
Previous Station – Whitechapel

Goal	Carriage	Door	Side
Exit	3	2	L

Stockwell

Northern — **No of Carriages = 6**

Direction From – North
Previous Station – Oval

Goal	Carriage	Door	Side
Exit	6	6	L
Victoria Line (South-Bound)	3	3	L
Victoria Line (South-Bound)	5	4	L
Victoria Line (South-Bound)	6	3	L
Victoria Line (North-Bound)	6	6	L

Direction From – South
Previous Station – Clapham North

Goal	Carriage	Door	Side
Exit	1	1	L
Victoria Line (North-Bound)	3	2	L
Victoria Line (North-Bound)	5	1/2	L
Victoria Line (South-Bound)	1	1	L

Stockwell *(cont...)*

Victoria **No of Carriages = 8**

Direction From – North
Previous Station – Vauxhall

Goal	Carriage	Door	Side
Exit	7	1	R
Northern (North-Bound)	7	1	R
Northern (South-Bound)	7	1	R
Northern (South-Bound)	4	3	R
Northern (South-Bound)	3	2	R

Direction From – South
Previous Station – Brixton

Goal	Carriage	Door	Side
Exit	1	3	R
Northern (North-Bound)	2	1	R
Northern (North-Bound)	3	2	R
Northern (North-Bound)	4	2	R
Northern (South-Bound)	1	3	R

Stonebridge Park

Bakerloo **No of Carriages = 7**

Direction From – North
Previous Station – Wembley Central

Goal	Carriage	Door	Side
Exit	2	1	L

Direction From – South
Previous Station – Harlesden

Goal	Carriage	Door	Side
Exit	7	3	L

Stratford

Central **No of Carriages = 8**

Direction From – East
Previous Station – Leyton

Goal	Carriage	Door	Side
DLR	2	3	R
Exit	3	3	R
Jubilee	2	3	R
Lift	1	1	R
Rail	3	3	R

Direction From – West
Previous Station – Mile End

Goal	Carriage	Door	Side
DLR	8	2	R
Exit	5	2	R
Jubilee	8	2	R
Lift	8	3	R
Rail	5	2	R

Jubilee *(Terminus)* **No of Carriages = 7**
Direction From – South
Previous Station – West Ham

Goal	Carriage	Door	Side
Exit	1	1	L/R
Rail	1	1	L/R

Sudbury Hill

Piccadilly **No of Carriages = 6**
Direction From – North
Previous Station – South Harrow

Goal	Carriage	Door	Side
Exit	2	2	L

Direction From – South
Previous Station – Sudbury Town

Goal	Carriage	Door	Side
Exit	5	2/3	L

Sudbury Town

Piccadilly **No of Carriages = 6**
Direction From – North
Previous Station – Sudbury Hill

Goal	Carriage	Door	Side
Exit	4	2	L

Direction From – South
Previous Station – Alperton

Goal	Carriage	Door	Side
Exit	3	3	L

Swiss Cottage

Jubilee **No of Carriages = 7**

Direction From – North

Previous Station – Finchley Road

Goal	Carriage	Door	Side
Exit	6	1	R

Direction From – South

Previous Station – St. John's Wood

Goal	Carriage	Door	Side
Exit	2	3	R

Temple

Circle **No of Carriages = 6**

Direction From – East

Previous Station – Blackfriars

Goal	Carriage	Door	Side
Exit	6	3	L

Direction From – West

Previous Station – Embankment

Goal	Carriage	Door	Side
Exit	2	1	L

District **No of Carriages = 6**

Direction From – East

Previous Station – Embankment

Goal	Carriage	Door	Side
Exit	5	4	L

Direction From – West

Previous Station – Temple

Goal	Carriage	Door	Side
Exit	2	2	L

Theydon Bois

Central **No of Carriages = 8**

Direction From – East

Previous Station – Epping

Goal	Carriage	Door	Side
Exit	5	1	L

Direction From – West
Previous Station – Debden

Goal	Carriage	Door	Side
Exit (via Footbridge)	5	3	L

Tooting Bec

Northern **No of Carriages = 6**

Direction From – North
Previous Station – Balham

Goal	Carriage	Door	Side
Exit	3	2	R

Direction From – South
Previous Station – Tooting Broadway

Goal	Carriage	Door	Side
Exit	3	4	R

Tooting Broadway

Northern **No of Carriages = 6**

Direction From – North
Previous Station – Tooting Bec

Goal	Carriage	Door	Side
Exit	3	2	R
Exit	4	2	R

Direction From – South
Previous Station – Colliers Wood

Goal	Carriage	Door	Side
Exit	2	4	R
Exit	3	4	R

Tottenham Court Road

Central **No of Carriages = 8**

Direction From – East
Previous Station – Holborn

Goal	Carriage	Door	Side
Exit	7	1	R
Exit	8	3	R
Northern	8	2	R

Tottenham Court Road *(cont...)*

Central **No of Carriages = 8**

Direction From – West
Previous Station – Oxford Circus

Goal	Carriage	Door	Side
Exit	1	1	R
Exit	3	3	R
Northern	1	1	R

Northern **No of Carriages = 6**

Direction From – North
Previous Station – Goodge Street

Goal	Carriage	Door	Side
Exit	3	4	R
Exit	5	4	R
Central	3	4	R
Central	5	4	R

Direction From – South
Previous Station – Leicester Square

Goal	Carriage	Door	Side
Exit	1	1	R
Exit	3	2	R
Central	1	1	R
Central	3	2	R

Tottenham Hale

Victoria **No of Carriages = 8**

Direction From – North
Previous Station – Blackhorse Road

Goal	Carriage	Door	Side
Exit	4	3	R
Exit (Lift)	8	3	R
Rail	4	3	R

Direction From – South
Previous Station – Seven Sisters

Goal	Carriage	Door	Side
Exit	5	1	R
Exit (Lift)	2	1	R
Rail	5	1	R

Totteridge & Whetstone

Northern **No of Carriages = 6**

Direction From – North
Previous Station – High Barnet

Goal	Carriage	Door	Side
Exit	1	3	L

Direction From – South
Previous Station – Woodside Park

Goal	Carriage	Door	Side
Exit	6	4	L

Tower Hill

Circle **No of Carriages = 6**

Direction From – East
Previous Station – Aldgate
Platform 1

Goal	Carriage	Door	Side
District (Eastwards)	6	2	R
District (Westwards)	Any	Any	R
Exit	6	2	R

Direction From – West
Previous Station – Monument
Platform 3

Goal	Carriage	Door	Side
District	Any	Any	L
Exit	3	3	L

District **No of Carriages = 6**

Direction From – East
Previous Station – Aldgate East

Goal	Carriage	Door	Side
Circle(Towards Monument)	Any	Any	R
Exit	5	3	R
Circle(Towards Aldgate)	2	3	R
Exit	2	3	R

Direction From – West
Previous Station – Monument

Goal	Carriage	Door	Side
Circle (Towards Algate)	Any	Any	L
Exit	2	3	L

Tufnell Park

Northern **No of Carriages = 6**

Direction From – North
Previous Station – Archway

Goal	Carriage	Door	Side
Exit	3	4	L

Direction From – South
Previous Station – Kentish Town

Goal	Carriage	Door	Side
Exit	4	4	R

Turnham Green

District **No of Carriages = 6**

Direction From – East
Previous Station – Stamford Brook

Goal	Carriage	Door	Side
Exit	2	1	R
Piccadilly (Eastwards)	2	1	R
Piccadilly (Westwards)	Any	Any	R

Direction From – West/South
Previous Station – Chiswick Park/Gunnersbury

Goal	Carriage	Door	Side
District (to South/West)	5	4	R
Exit	5	4	R
Piccadilly (Eastwards)	Any	Any	R
Piccadilly (Westwards)	5	4	R

Piccadilly **No of Carriages = 6**

(Only before 6:50 {7:50 Sundays} & after 22:30)

Direction From – East
Previous Station – Hammersmith

Goal	Carriage	Door	Side
District (Eastwards)	2	4	L
District (Westwards)	Any	Any	L
Exit	2	4	L

Direction From – West
Previous Station – Acton Town

Goal	Carriage	Door	Side
District (Eastwards)	Any	Any	L
District (South/Westwards)	5	4	L
Exit	5	4	L

Turnpike Lane

Piccadilly **No of Carriages = 6**

Direction From – North
Previous Station – Wood Green

Goal	Carriage	Door	Side
Exit	2	4	R

Direction From – South
Previous Station – Manor House

Goal	Carriage	Door	Side
Exit	4	4	R

Upminster *(Terminus)*

District **No of Carriages = 6**

Direction From – South
Previous Station – Upminster Bridge
Platforms 3 & 4

Goal	Carriage	Door	Side
Exit & Rail	6	2	L/R
Lift	6	4	L/R
Platform 5			
Exit & Rail	5	4	R
Lift	6	4	R

Upminster Bridge

District **No of Carriages = 6**

Direction From – East
Previous Station – Upminster

Goal	Carriage	Door	Side
Exit	6	4	R

Direction From – West
Previous Station – Hornchurch

Goal	Carriage	Door	Side
Exit	1	1	R

Upney

District — **No of Carriages = 6**

Direction From – East
Previous Station – Becontree

Goal	Carriage	Door	Side
Exit	6	4	R

Direction From – West
Previous Station – Barking

Goal	Carriage	Door	Side
Exit	1	1	R

Upton Park

District — **No of Carriages = 6**

Direction From – East
Previous Station – East Ham

Goal	Carriage	Door	Side
Exit	6	4	L

Direction From – West
Previous Station – Plaistow

Goal	Carriage	Door	Side
Exit	1	1	L

Hammersmith & City — **No of Carriages = 6**

Direction From – East
Previous Station – East Ham

Goal	Carriage	Door	Side
Exit	6	4	L

Direction From – West
Previous Station – Plaistow

Goal	Carriage	Door	Side
Exit	1	1	L

Uxbridge *(Terminus)*

Metropolitan — **No of Carriages = 8**

Direction From – East
Previous Station – Hillingdon

Goal	Carriage	Door	Side
Exit	1	1	L/R

Piccadilly **No of Carriages = 6**

Direction From – East
Previous Station – Hillingdon

Goal	Carriage	Door	Side
Exit	1	1	L/R

Vauxhall

Victoria **No of Carriages = 8**

Direction From – North
Previous Station – Victoria

Goal	Carriage	Door	Side
Exit	5	3	R
Rail	5	3	R

Direction From – South
Previous Station – Stockwell

Goal	Carriage	Door	Side
Exit	3	3	R
Rail	3	3	R

Victoria

District & **Circle** **No of Carriages = 6**

Direction From – East
Previous Station – St. James's Park

Goal	Carriage	Door	Side
Exit	2	1	L
Exit	4	1	L
Rail	2	1	L
Rail	4	1	L
Victoria	6	3	L

Direction From – West
Previous Station – Sloane Square

Goal	Carriage	Door	Side
Exit	6	2	L
Rail	6	2	L
Victoria	2	3	L

Victoria *(cont...)*

Victoria **No of Carriages = 8**

Direction From – North
Previous Station – Green Park

Goal	Carriage	Door	Side
Circle	5	1	R
District	5	1	R
Exit	1	1	R
Rail	1	1	R

Direction From – South
Previous Station – Vauxhall

Goal	Carriage	Door	Side
Circle	4	2/3	R
District	4	2/3	R
Exit	4	2/3	R
Rail	4	2/3	R

Walthamstow Central *(Terminus)*

Victoria **No of Carriages = 8**

Direction From – South
Previous Station – Blackhorse Road

Goal	Carriage	Door	Side
Exit	1	3	L/R
Rail	1	3	L/R

Wanstead

Central **No of Carriages = 8**

Direction From – East
Previous Station – Redbridge

Goal	Carriage	Door	Side
Exit	4	2	R

Direction From – West
Previous Station – Leytonstone

Goal	Carriage	Door	Side
Exit	5	4	R

Warren Street

Northern — **No of Carriages = 6**

Direction From – North
Previous Station – Euston

Goal	Carriage	Door	Side
Exit	6	3	L
Victoria	6	3	L

Direction From – South
Previous Station – Goodge Street

Goal	Carriage	Door	Side
Exit	2	2	L
Victoria	2	2	L

Victoria — **No of Carriages = 8**

Direction From – North
Previous Station – Euston

Goal	Carriage	Door	Side
Exit	4	3	L
Northern	4	3	L

Direction From – South
Previous Station – Oxford Circus

Goal	Carriage	Door	Side
Exit	4	2	L
Northern	4	2	L

Warwick Avenue

Bakerloo — **No of Carriages = 7**

Direction From – North
Previous Station – Maida Vale

Goal	Carriage	Door	Side
Exit	5	1	R

Direction From – South
Previous Station – Paddington

Goal	Carriage	Door	Side
Exit	3	2/3	R

Waterloo

Bakerloo **No of Carriages = 7**

Direction From – North
Previous Station – Embankment

Goal	Carriage	Door	Side
Exit (S. Bank)	6	3	L
Exit	5	2	L
Jubilee	6	3	L
Northern	4	2	L
Northern	6	3	L
Rail	3	2	L
Rail	4	2	L
Rail	5	2	L
Waterloo & City	4	2	L

Direction From – South
Previous Station – Lambeth North

Goal	Carriage	Door	Side
Exit	1	2	R
Exit (S. Bank)	2	3	R
Jubilee	2	3	R
Northern	2	3	R
Rail	2	3	R
Waterloo & City	2	3	R

Jubilee **No of Carriages = 7**

Direction From –North
Previous Station – Westminster

Goal	Carriage	Door	Side
Bakerloo	1	4	R
Bakerloo	5	4	R
Exit	1	4	R
Exit	5	4	R
Lift	4	2	R
Northern	1	4	R
Northern	5	4	R
Rail	1	4	R
Rail	5	4	R
Waterloo & City	1	4	R
Waterloo & City	5	4	R

Direction From – South
Previous Station – Southwark

Goal	Carriage	Door	Side
Bakerloo	1	1	R
Bakerloo	7	4	R
Exit	1	1	R
Exit	7	4	R
Lift	4	3	R
Northern	1	1	R
Northern	7	4	R
Rail	1	1	R
Rail	7	4	R
Waterloo & City	1	1	R
Waterloo & City	7	4	R

Northern **No of Carriages = 6**
Direction From – North
Previous Station – Embankment

Goal	Carriage	Door	Side
Bakerloo	3	4	R
Exit	4	4	R
Jubilee	5	3	R
Rail	3	4	R
South Bank	4	4	R
Waterloo & City	3	4	R

Direction From – South
Previous Station – Kennington

Goal	Carriage	Door	Side
Bakerloo	3	3	R
Exit	1	3	R
Jubilee	3	3	R
Rail	3	3	R
South Bank	2	3	R
Waterloo & City	3	3	R

Waterloo *(cont...)*

Waterloo & City **No of Carriages = 4**
Direction From – East
Previous Station – Bank

Goal	Carriage	Door	Side
Exit	1	1	L/R
Jubilee	1	1	L/R
Northern	1	1	L/R
Bakerloo	1	1	L/R
Rail	1	1	L/R

Watford *(Terminus)*

Metropolitan **No of Carriages = 8**
Direction From – South
Previous Station – Croxley

Goal	Carriage	Door	Side
Exit	1	1	L/R

Wembley Central

Bakerloo **No of Carriages = 7**
Direction From – North
Previous Station – North Wembley

Goal	Carriage	Door	Side
Exit	6	3/4	L
Rail	6	3/4	L

Direction From – South
Previous Station – Stonebridge Park

Goal	Carriage	Door	Side
Exit	2	2	L
Rail	2	2	L

Wembley Park

Jubilee

No of Carriages = 7

Direction From – North
Previous Station – Kingsbury

Goal	Carriage	Door	Side
Exit	2	2	L
Exit	4	1	L
Exit	5	2	L
Lift	1	1	L
Metropolitan	Any	Any	L

Direction From – South
Previous Station – Neasden

Goal	Carriage	Door	Side
Exit	6	1	L
Exit	4	3	L
Exit	2	3	L
Lift	6	4	L
Metropolitan	Any	Any	L

Metropolitan

No of Carriages = 8

Direction From – North
Previous Station – Preston Road

Goal	Carriage	Door	Side
Exit	3	1	L/R
Exit	4	3	L/R
Exit	6	2	L/R
Jubilee	3	1	L/R
Jubilee	4	3	L/R
Jubilee	6	2	L/R

Direction From – South
Previous Station – South Hampstead

Platform 1

Goal	Carriage	Door	Side
Exit	3	3	L
Exit	7	1	L
Jubilee	3	3	L
Jubilee	7	1	L

Wembley Park *(cont...)*

Metropolitan *cont...)* **No of Carriages = 8**

Direction From – South
Previous Station – South Hampstead
Platform 2

Goal	Carriage	Door	Side
Exit	3	2	R
Exit	5	1	R
Exit	7	2	R
Jubilee (Northwards)	Any	Any	R

West Acton

Central **No of Carriages = 8**

Direction From – East
Previous Station – North Acton

Goal	Carriage	Door	Side
Exit	1	2	L

Direction From – West
Previous Station – Ealing

Goal	Carriage	Door	Side
Exit	8	2	L

West Brompton

District **No of Carriages = 6**

Direction From – North
Previous Station – Earl's Court
Platform 2

Goal	Carriage	Door	Side
Exit	6	4	L
Rail	6	4	L

Direction From – South
Previous Station – Fulham Broadway
Platform 1

Goal	Carriage	Door	Side
Exit	2	L	
Exit	2	4	L
Lift (only this Platform)	3	2	L
Rail	3	3	L

West Finchley

Northern **No of Carriages = 6**

Direction From – North
Previous Station – Woodside Park

Goal	Carriage	Door	Side
Exit	6	4	R
Lift	6	4	R

Direction From – South
Previous Station – Finchley Central

Goal	Carriage	Door	Side
Exit	2	2	R
Lift	2	2	R

West Ham

District **No of Carriages = 6**

Direction From – East
Previous Station – Plaistow

Goal	Carriage	Door	Side
Exit	1	1	R
Jubilee	1	1	R
Rail	1	1	R

Direction From – West
Previous Station – Bromley-by Bow

Goal	Carriage	Door	Side
Exit	6	4	R
Jubilee	6	4	R
Rail	6	4	R

Hammersmith & City **No of Carriages = 6**

Direction From – East
Previous Station – Plaistow

Goal	Carriage	Door	Side
Exit	1	1	R
Jubilee	1	1	R
Rail	1	1	R

West Ham *(cont...)*

Hammersmith & City *(cont...)* **No of Carriages = 6**

Direction From – West
Previous Station – Bromley-by Bow

Goal	Carriage	Door	Side
Exit	6	4	R
Jubilee	6	4	R
Rail	6	4	R

Jubilee **No of Carriages = 7**

Direction From – North
Previous Station – Stratford

Goal	Carriage	Door	Side
District	5	2	R
Exit	5	2	R
Hammersmith & City	5	2	R
Lift	3	3	R

Direction From – South
Previous Station – Canning Town

Goal	Carriage	Door	Side
District	3	2	R
Exit	3	2	R
Hammersmith & City	3	2	R
Lift	5	2	R

West Hampstead

Jubilee **No of Carriages = 7**

Direction From – North
Previous Station – Kilburn

Goal	Carriage	Door	Side
Exit	7	4	R
Rail	7	4	R

Direction From – South
Previous Station – Finchley Road

Goal	Carriage	Door	Side
Exit	1	1	R
Rail	1	1	R

West Harrow

Metropolitan **No of Carriages = 8**

Direction From – East
Previous Station – Harrow-on-the Hill

Goal	Carriage	Door	Side
Exit	8	1	L

Direction From – West
Previous Station – Rayners Lane

Goal	Carriage	Door	Side
Exit	2	2	L

West Kensington

District **No of Carriages = 6**

Direction From – East
Previous Station – Earl's Court

Goal	Carriage	Door	Side
Exit	1	1	L

Direction From – West
Previous Station – Barons Court

Goal	Carriage	Door	Side
Exit	6	1	L

West Ruislip *(Terminus)*

Central **No of Carriages = 8**

Direction From – South
Previous Station – Ruislip Gardens

Goal	Carriage	Door	Side
Rail	1	2	L/R
Exit	1	2	L/R

Westbourne Park

Circle **No of Carriages = 6**

Direction From – East
Previous Station – Royal Oak

Goal	Carriage	Door	Side
Exit	6	4	L
Hammersmith & City	Any	Any	L

Direction From – West
Previous Station – Ladbroke Grove

Goal	Carriage	Door	Side
Exit	1	3	L
Hammersmith & City	Any	Any	L

Hammersmith & City **No of Carriages = 6**

Direction From – East
Previous Station – Royal Oak

Goal	Carriage	Door	Side
Circle	Any	Any	L
Exit	6	4	L

Direction From – West
Previous Station – Ladbroke Grove

Goal	Carriage	Door	Side
Circle	Any	Any	L
Exit	1	3	L

Westminster

District **&** **Circle** **No of Carriages = 6**

Direction From – East
Previous Station – Embankment

Goal	Carriage	Door	Side
Exit	3	4	L
Jubilee	3	4	L
Lift (Exit)	4	2	L
Lift (Jubilee)	3	4	L

Direction From – West
Previous Station – St. James's Park

Goal	Carriage	Door	Side
Exit	5	4	L
Jubilee	4	4	L
Lift (Exit & Jubilee)	4	2	L

Jubilee **No of Carriages = 7**

Direction From – North
Previous Station – Green Park

Goal	Carriage	Door	Side
District & Circle	1	3	L
Exit	4	2	L
Lift	1	3	L
Lift	4	3	L

Direction From – South
Previous Station – Waterloo

Goal	Carriage	Door	Side
District & Circle	4	3	R
Exit	6	1/2	R
Lift	6	1/2	R

White City

Central **No of Carriages = 8**

Direction From – East
Previous Station – Shepherd's Bush

Goal	Carriage	Door	Side
Exit	3	1	L/R
Exit	5	2	L/R

Direction From – East *and Terminates*
Previous Station – Shepherd's Bush

Goal	Carriage	Door	Side
Exit	2	4	L
Exit	3	1	L

Direction From – West
Previous Station – East Acton

Goal	Carriage	Door	Side
Exit	4	3	L
Exit	7	1	L

Whitechapel

District **No of Carriages = 6**

Direction From – East
Previous Station – Stepney Green

Goal	Carriage	Door	Side
Exit	6	4	L
Rail	6	1	L

Direction From – West
Previous Station – Aldgate East

Goal	Carriage	Door	Side
Exit	1	1	L/R
Rail	1	1	L/R

Hammersmith & City **No of Carriages = 6**

Direction From – East
Previous Station – Stepney Green

Goal	Carriage	Door	Side
Exit	6	4	L/R
Rail	6	4	L/R

Direction From – West
Previous Station – Aldgate East

Goal	Carriage	Door	Side
Exit	1	1	L/R
Rail	2	2	L/R

Willesden Green

Jubilee **No of Carriages = 7**

Direction From – North
Previous Station – Dollis Hill

Goal	Carriage	Door	Side
Exit	1	3	R

Direction From – South
Previous Station – Kilburn

Goal	Carriage	Door	Side
Exit	5	2	R

Willesden Junction

Bakerloo **No of Carriages = 7**

Direction From – North
Previous Station – Harlesden

Goal	Carriage	Door	Side
Exit	1	1	R
Rail	Any	Any	R

Direction From – South
Previous Station – Kensal Green

Goal	Carriage	Door	Side
Exit	7	3	R
Rail	Any	Any	

Wimbledon *(Terminus)*

District **No of Carriages = 6**

Direction From – North
Previous Station – Wimbledon Park

Goal	Carriage	Door	Side
Exit	1	1	L/R
Rail	1	1	L/R

Wimbledon Park

District **No of Carriages = 6**

Direction From – North
Previous Station – Southfields

Goal	Carriage	Door	Side
Exit	6	4	R

Direction From – South
Previous Station – Wimbledon

Goal	Carriage	Door	Side
Exit	1	3	R

Wood Green

Piccadilly **No of Carriages = 6**

Direction From – North
Previous Station – Bounds Green

Goal	Carriage	Door	Side
Ex it	4	3	R

Direction From – South
Previous Station – Turnpike Lane

Goal	Carriage	Door	Side
Exit	3	1	R

Wood Lane

Circle **No of Carriages = 6**

Direction From – North
Previous Station – Latimer Road

Goal	Carriage	Door	Side
Central (White City)	2	2	L
Exit	2	2	L
Hammersmith & City	Any	Any	L
Lift	1	1	L

Direction From – South
Previous Station – Shepherd's Bush Market

Goal	Carriage	Door	Side
Central (White City)	5	1	L
Exit	5	1	L
Hammersmith & City	Any	Any	L
Lift	6	4	L

Hammersmith & City **No of Carriages = 6**

Direction From – North
Previous Station – Latimer Road

Goal	Carriage	Door	Side
Central (White City)	2	2	L
Circle	Any	Any	L
Exit	2	2	L
Lift	1	1	L

Direction From – South
Previous Station – Shepherd's Bush Market

Goal	Carriage	Door	Side
Central (White City)	5	1	L
Circle	Any	Any	L
Exit	5	1	L
Lift	6	4	L

Woodford

Central **No of Carriages = 8**

Direction From – North
Previous Station – Buckhurst Hill/Roding Valley

Goal	Carriage	Door	Side
Branch to Roding Valley	8	3	R
Exit	8	3	R
Exit (The Broadway)	6	2	R

Direction From – South
Previous Station – South Woodford

Goal	Carriage	Door	Side
Branch to Roding Valley	Any	Any	L
Exit	1	1	L

Woodside Park

Northern **No of Carriages = 6**

Direction From – North
Previous Station – Totteridge & Whetstone

Goal	Carriage	Door	Side
Exit	3	4	L
Lift	3	4	L

Direction From – South
Previous Station – West Finchley

Goal	Carriage	Door	Side
Exit	2	3	L
Lift	2	3	L

FIN

ND - #0250 - 080726 - C152 - 148/105/13 - PB - 9781780355641 - Gloss Lamination